Life After Work

How to Have the Fulfilling Retirement You Deserve, Full of Purpose, Laughter, and Things You Actually Want to Do

P. Alexander

LITTLE AP PUBLISHING

ISBN: 979-8-871-98270-9

LIFE AFTER WORK

Contents

INTRODUCTION

The company gave me an aptitude test, and I found out the work I was best suited for was retirement. –Unknown

Retirement—a word that carries a multitude of meanings, aspirations, and, perhaps, a touch of anxiety. It's a juncture in life that beckons with the promise of freedom and newfound adventures, yet it can also stir up a whirlwind of emotions, leaving us grappling with uncertainties and insecurities. For many, the transition from a structured work life to the uncharted waters of retirement is a leap into the unknown, laden with both excitement and trepidation.

As the pages of our working years flip over to reveal the blank canvas of retirement, it's only natural to wonder: Have we prepared enough for this? Are we truly ready to bid adieu to the routines we've grown accustomed to? Will our finances support the dreams we've nurtured for this phase of life? These questions often punctuate our thoughts, injecting a slight feeling of unease into what should ideally be a joyous leap into a well-earned respite.

But let's pause for a moment and acknowledge something very human: the struggle and anxiety that can accompany this significant life transition. Retirement is a shift, both in lifestyle and mindset. It's a departure from the familiar, a departure from the routine that has defined us for so long. It's a shift from being consumed by deadlines and meetings to having the luxury of more free hours. Yet, this very prospect can become a double-edged sword—freedom tinged with worry as we grapple with the vast expanse of time and the responsibility of managing it well.

In an article published by CNBC, the statistics remind us that a considerable number of individuals start saving for retirement later than they believe they should. This revelation is not meant to induce panic or regret; instead, it's a gentle nudge, a reminder that you're not alone in your journey. The path to retirement is rarely a straight line, and the starting point matters less than the steps you take from this point forward.

The book's purpose here is not to accentuate the fear of being "late" to the retirement planning party. Quite the opposite. It's here to reassure, to affirm, and to guide you through this exciting chapter.

The Adjustment Period

It's important to recognize that adjusting to retirement is a process, and like any significant life change, it takes time and patience. First and foremost, allow yourself to acknowledge the shift. Embrace it as a new beginning, a chance to reinvent your daily routine, and an opportunity to explore your passions and interests. One of the joys of retirement is having the freedom to rediscover what truly brings you happiness. Whether it's painting, hiking, gardening, or learning a new language, now is the time to reignite the flames of your passions. Engaging in activities that ignite your spirit will not only fill your days but also provide a sense of purpose and fulfillment.

While retirement may mean bidding farewell to a rigid work schedule, it doesn't diminish the importance of structure in your day. Establish a flexible routine that includes activities you enjoy, time for relaxation, exercise, and social interactions. This routine will give your days a sense of direction and prevent them from blurring into an indistinct haze. The freedom of retirement also provides you with the opportunity to break out of your isolation to connect with others and strengthen bonds of friendship.

Retirement, though often accompanied by uncertainties and adjustments, should be celebrated as a milestone—a culmination of hard work, dedication, and a life well-lived. This is your time to reap the rewards, to relish the freedom, and to bask in the joy of a well-deserved break from the conventional. This phase of life invites us to pause and reflect on our life's journey so far. It's a chance to celebrate your achievements, the challenges you've overcome, and the wisdom you've gained along the way. Consider it a well-earned intermission before the next act, where you get to rewrite the script according to your desires.

In the whirlwind of our professional lives, we tend to overlook the simple joys that make life beautiful. Retirement encourages us to slow down and savor these little pleasures—like a leisurely walk in the park, a cup of coffee with a friend, or a good book on a quiet afternoon. It's about appreciating the now and finding happiness in the small, everyday moments. All of these experiences just scratch the surface of all that you have to look forward to in retirement. However, in the spirit of fairness and holistic thinking, we also have to talk about the elephant(s) in the room.

Not All Sunshine and Rainbows

Yes, retirement is a monumental life event, and with it comes a host of concerns and worries. It's essential to acknowledge and understand these concerns to navigate this transition successfully. Starting retirement planning later than anticipated can lead to concerns about having enough time to save and invest for a comfortable retirement. The worry that time may not be on your side can be daunting, but it's never too late to take meaningful steps toward securing your future.

The fear of not having enough money to sustain the desired lifestyle during retirement is a significant concern. Financial security is a cornerstone of a fulfilling retirement, and uncertainty about financial stability can cast a shadow over what should be an exciting phase of life. On top of that, the world of retirement planning is often riddled with complex financial jargon and intricate concepts. This complexity can feel overwhelming and deter individuals from making informed decisions, leaving them unsure of how to navigate this complicated landscape. Understanding investment strategies, tax implications, and government benefits can be challenging. The lack of comprehensive knowledge in these areas can leave you uncertain about how to maximize your resources effectively. If you never took the time to learn these principles in your career, then you might be faced with a great deal of anxiety as you look into life after you're done working. And this is just the tip of the iceberg.

Unforeseen expenses, career setbacks, or simply not being able to save enough during your working years can lead to the worry of having inadequate retirement savings. It's a common concern, and many face the challenge of making their savings stretch through their retirement years. The rising costs of healthcare and potential medical expenses in retirement are a genuine cause for concern. Health is wealth, and addressing these worries is crucial to ensuring a well-rounded retirement plan.

This book is not about dismissing these anxieties; it's about acknowledging them and addressing them with practical advice, reassurance, and a light-hearted approach. We understand the worries that retirement can bring, and we're here to guide you through, offering solutions and empowering you to craft a retirement that aligns with your aspirations and dreams.

Preparation Is Key

With everything that we've already talked about so far, you might be feeling a little overwhelmed. That's perfectly normal. However, embarking on this journey with the right knowledge and guidance can transform the experience. This book takes a holistic approach to retirement, addressing not just the financial aspects but also the emotional, social, and lifestyle dimensions. By the end, you'll have a well-rounded understanding of the intricacies involved in planning for a fulfilling retirement. Yes, retirement can be scary sometimes. But it doesn't always have to be!

Each chapter of this book is designed to offer actionable advice and practical steps to tackle the challenges you may encounter during this phase. Whether it's financial planning, adjusting to a new routine, or finding purpose, this book equips you with the tools to face these hurdles head-on. By demystifying the complex financial jargon and explaining investment strategies, tax planning, and government benefits in simple terms, the contents of this book will empower you to make informed decisions with confidence. No more feeling lost in the world of financial planning.

However, it's important to understand that every individual's circumstances are unique. There is no one-size-fits-all approach to retirement planning. That's why the solutions to retirement planning should be as fluid and dynamic as possible. This book offers a range of strategies and solutions, allowing you to tailor your retirement plans to match your specific situation and aspirations.

Retirement should be looked upon as a new beginning, a chapter filled with excitement and joy. Together, we can inspire and motivate you to embrace this phase wholeheartedly, viewing it as an opportunity to craft the life you've always desired.

Looking Forward to Life After Work

Imagine a retirement where you wake up each day with a sense of purpose and excitement, where your financial worries are minimized, and where you have the freedom to pursue your passions and interests. Picture a life enriched with the warmth of family and friends and a deep satisfaction from your choices. This is the end result this book envisions for you—a retirement that's not just financially secure but emotionally, socially, and personally fulfilling.

There's no sugarcoating it. Navigating the complexities of retirement can be a challenging endeavor. There will be uncertainties, moments of doubt, and questions that seem to have elusive answers. But fear not, for this book is designed to make this journey as easy and as simple as possible. With every chapter, you will be provided with clear, logical guidance that's easy to follow and understand. We unravel the intricacies of retirement planning together, finding solutions to specific problems and challenges that you might face. There's no magic wand here, just practical advice that's rooted in reality. Ultimately, this book empowers you to take control of your retirement. It arms you with the knowledge to make informed decisions, giving you the confidence to navigate this phase with grace and resilience.

Life After Work is more than just a book—it's your companion, your confidant, and your guide through this exciting journey. Together, we'll transform your retirement from a source of worry into a realm of endless possibilities and joy.

Retirement - The Grand Adventure Begins

A lot of the time, people get the wrong idea of retirement. They see it as the finish line after a long and hard, grueling race. They picture retirement as a sigh of relief or a quiet retreat from the many years of working hard. But there's something much more to it than that. In fact, a study unearthed that 97% of retirees who embarked on this journey with a strong sense of purpose found themselves basking in happiness and satisfaction (Reed, 2022). This is not merely a statistic; it's a revelation—a testament to the transformative and fulfilling power of retirement.

Retirement is not a destination; it's the beginning of a grand adventure, a blank canvas waiting for you to paint with the vibrant colors of your dreams and desires. It's a phase where you have the privilege of redefining life on your own terms, unburdened by the constraints of a structured workday. This chapter is your doorway to understanding that retirement is more than a prolonged weekend or an extended vacation. It's a profound change that offers a unique opportunity—a chance to reforge your path, plan your time wisely, and address practical considerations. The statistics echo a profound truth: a sense of purpose in retirement can be your guiding light, illuminating a path filled with fulfillment, joy, and contentment.

Retirement as a New Chapter in Life

Retirement isn't merely the end of a professional career; it marks the commencement of a new and transformative chapter in your life. It's a profound change that touches the essence of who you are and how you navigate the world. Just as every chapter in a book contributes to the overarching story, so does retirement play a vital role in the tale of your life. As you step into retirement, you are embarking on a journey that is unlike any other. The structured days of the workplace are behind you, and a vast expanse of time stretches before you. This shift can be both exhilarating and daunting, beckoning you to explore uncharted territories while bidding adieu to the familiar rhythms of your career.

At its core, retirement is a time to rediscover your identity beyond your professional title. It's an opportunity to explore your passions, hobbies, and interests, unburdened by the demands of a nine-to-five routine. It's a period for self-discovery and self-reinvention—a time to ponder the legacy you wish to create and the experiences you want to embrace.

Forge Your Own Path

Just because retirement isn't an experience that is exclusively your own doesn't mean that you shouldn't make it unique! Even in retirement, the path you choose to take is yours to forge. Unlike the structured, predetermined course of a career, retirement allows you the unparalleled freedom to chart your own journey. It's your time to explore, take detours, and relish the scenic routes as you see fit.

This is the moment to contemplate the life you've always envisioned—a life that aligns with your dreams, interests, and passions. Forge your path with intention and enthusiasm, keeping in mind that there's no universal blueprint for retirement. It's an opportunity to mold your life to your liking, and the possibilities are as vast as your imagination. Embrace this notion of forging your own path with a sense of adventure. Whether it's embarking on a long-held dream of traveling the world, dedicating more time to a cherished hobby, or taking up entirely new pursuits, your choices are boundless. From volunteering to pursuing further education, every decision you make contributes to your unique retirement narrative.

To forge your own path, it's essential to consider what truly makes your heart sing. What are the activities, interests, and passions that ignite your spirit? This could be a creative hobby, a meaningful cause, or simply a leisurely stroll in the park. As you consider these aspects, you'll begin to shape a retirement that reflects your values and aspirations. Throughout this process, it's imperative that you stay open to new experiences and changes in direction. The beauty of this phase is its flexibility, allowing you to adapt and pivot as you discover new interests or encounter unforeseen opportunities.

Be Mindful of Your Time

One of the greatest gifts that retirement affords you is the gift of time. With this time, you get more freedom to design your daily life according to your aspirations and interests. However, this newfound freedom can be a double-edged sword if not managed thoughtfully.

Planning how to spend your time in retirement is not about turning your days into rigorously scheduled agendas. Rather, it's about crafting a life that balances relaxation and productivity. It's the art of designing your days to align with everything you want to accomplish and pursue for the rest of your life. Here are a few tips on how you can make the most out of your time in retirement:

Retirement doesn't mean retiring from life itself. It's a time to find a new sense of purpose. Consider how you can channel your skills, talents, and interests into meaningful activities. Volunteering, mentoring, or pursuing a long-nurtured passion can infuse your days with a sense of fulfillment.

Take this opportunity to delve deeper into hobbies or interests you might have put on hold during your working years. Whether it's playing a musical instrument, gardening, or learning a new language, these pursuits can be a source of joy and personal growth.

Physical activity is a cornerstone of a healthy retirement. Regular exercise not only keeps you physically fit but also boosts mental well-being. Find an activity you enjoy, whether it's daily walks, swimming, yoga, or joining a fitness class.

Retirement can sometimes lead to feelings of isolation, particularly if you've left behind a bustling workplace. Actively seek social connections, whether through community activities, joining clubs, or maintaining strong relationships with friends and family.

Remember that retirement isn't just about leisure; it's also about finding a work-life balance that suits your preferences. This may involve part-time work, consulting, or freelancing, allowing you to stay engaged while enjoying more flexibility.

Retirement offers the perfect opportunity for travel and exploration. Whether crossing destinations off your bucket list or discovering hidden gems in your backyard, adventure is calling.

Again, retirement doesn't have to look the same for everyone. So, when you're in the process of determining how you want to spend your time, stay flexible. That's really the key to making the most out of this phase of your life. The ability to adapt and change your plans as new interests and opportunities arise ensures that your retirement remains an evolving and exciting chapter in your life.

Always Be Practical

By now, after everything that we've discussed, you're probably feeling hyped up and excited about retirement. However, in the midst of all this excitement, it's still important to stay grounded in reality. While retirement brings the promise of newfound freedom and opportunities, it also comes with a set of practical considerations that are essential to address. These are the realities that, when thoughtfully managed, can contribute to a smooth and fulfilling retirement.

Financial Stability: Maintaining financial stability is a top priority. This includes assessing your retirement savings, budgeting for your new lifestyle, and considering any additional sources of income, such as pension or part-time work.

Healthcare and Insurance: Healthcare is a significant concern in retirement. Ensure you have a comprehensive health insurance plan and understand how it works. Factor in potential healthcare costs, such as premiums, copayments, and medications.

Estate Planning: Estate planning involves ensuring your assets are managed and distributed according to your wishes. This includes creating or updating your will, designating beneficiaries, and considering any tax implications.

Social Security: Understanding how and when to claim Social Security benefits is crucial. Decisions in this area can significantly impact your financial well-being in retirement.

Family and Caregiving: Some retirees may find themselves as caregivers for aging parents or family members. It's important to plan for the potential responsibilities and financial implications that come with caregiving.

Housing: Housing is also an important consideration for retirees. How big should your future living arrangement be? Will you be going for assisted living at a care facility? Will you continue to live on your own or with other family? Knowing what your future living arrangements could look like will allow you to better prepare for them.

Travel and Leisure Activities: Plan how you'll allocate your time for travel, leisure, and recreation. This may involve setting aside a budget for vacations, joining clubs, or participating in activities that interest you.

Legal Matters: This includes updating important legal documents, such as powers of attorney and healthcare directives. Having these documents in order can provide peace of mind for you and your loved ones.

As you delve into the practical aspects of retirement, it's important to seek guidance where needed. Consulting with financial advisors, estate planning experts, and legal professionals can provide valuable insights and ensure you've covered all essential bases. Also, seek the perspective of your family and loved ones. They can help provide more context for your retirement that you might have missed on your own.

The Importance of Staying Active and Fit

Retirement is not just a time for rest; it's an opportunity to engage your mind and stay mentally active. Keeping your mental faculties sharp is essential for a fulfilling and enriching retirement. One of the most common mistakes that retirees make is to just kick back, relax, and forget about the world. Yes, there is value in being able to rest and rejuvenate. But sitting around and doing nothing can lead to significant cognitive decline. On top of that, spending prolonged hours sitting can lead to various health concerns, including weight gain, heart problems, and a decline in cognitive function. It's crucial to understand the risks associated with excessive sedentary time and take steps to counteract them. In this section, we'll explore the various ways you can stay active even while in retirement.

Staying Physically Active: Exercise is not only vital for your physical health but also a potent tool for keeping your mind sharp. The key is to find physical activities that genuinely interest you. Whether hiking, dancing, swimming, or even regular walks, engaging in activities you enjoy makes exercise a pleasure, not a chore.

Keeping Up With Housework: A tidy living space isn't just aesthetically pleasing; it's also conducive to mental clarity. Household chores offer a sense of accomplishment and a visually pleasing environment.

Developing a Green Thumb: Gardening is more than a pastime; it's a therapeutic and mentally stimulating activity. Tending to plants, whether in a small balcony garden or a larger backyard plot, offers a range of cognitive and emotional benefits.

Refining Your Eating Habits: A balanced diet is not only essential for physical health but also plays a significant role in maintaining cognitive acuity. What you eat can impact memory, concentration, and overall mental well-being.

Prioritizing Family Time: Retirement is a grand ole time for family connections. Spending quality time with family members can bring joy and emotional well-being.

Again, there are so many ways you can go about to sharpen your physical and mental acuity. Retirement doesn't mean you are doing nothing for the rest of your life. Go ahead and read all the books that have been on your *to-be-read* list for a while now. Do crossword puzzles and other mental activities that will stimulate your brain. Research topics and interests that you might be interested in. Enroll in classes or courses that will fill your brain with knowledge about things you're curious about. Spend your time listening to music or podcasts about topics that you enjoy. Watch YouTube videos or even dabble in content creation yourself! The point here is that the world is filled with endless possibilities of ways for you to spend your time constructively. Don't sell yourself short, and experience as many of these things as possible!

Retirement as a Second Life

To end this chapter, I want you to read about a story that's more grounded in reality. Everything that we've talked about so far is theoretical, as you have yet to apply these things in your life. But I want to tell you about Alvin, the dad of a very good friend of mine, who is very much in the thick of his retirement. Alvin's journey into retirement was not just about ending his career but also about opening a new, vibrant chapter filled with passion, purpose, and adventure.

For Alvin, retirement marked a well-earned break from a demanding career in engineering. As he bid farewell to the daily grind of the corporate world, he faced the same questions and uncertainties that many retirees encounter. What would he do with all his free time? How would he find purpose beyond his professional identity? How could he ensure that his retirement years were not just a quiet retreat but a grand adventure?

After mulling it over for a bit, he decided to pursue his long-held passion for photography. With a camera in hand and a thirst for exploration, he set out to capture the beauty of the world around him. Photography became a newfound source of joy and creativity, allowing him to not only capture stunning images but also connect with the communities he encountered on his journeys.

Alvin's story illustrates that retirement is not the end of the road but the beginning of an incredible journey. It's an opportunity to reignite passions, explore new horizons, and give back to the community. Alvin's retirement is a testament to the fact that it's never too late to pursue your dreams and that every day in retirement is a chance to live life to the fullest.

Now, you don't exactly have to have a story like Alvin's, and that's not a bad thing! You get to make a story that's entirely your own and one that you can be proud of.

Chapter Conclusion

If there's one key takeaway that you should have from this chapter, it's this: Retirement is not merely the end of a career but the beginning of a new phase—a phase filled with promises, passions, and endless possibilities.

We've discussed the importance of recognizing retirement as a momentous change, forging your unique path, planning how to spend your time wisely, and addressing the practical considerations that ensure your retirement is both fulfilling and secure. This chapter has provided a foundation for you to embark on your retirement journey with wisdom and enthusiasm.

As we move forward with the book, we will now be tackling more specific aspects of your second life, particularly when it comes to revamping your wardrobe. We'll explore how to align your attire with your retirement lifestyle, emphasizing the importance of comfort without compromising style.

FROM SUITS TO PAJAMAS - THE WARDROBE TRANSITION

When we think of retirement, the image that often comes to mind is one of leisure, comfort, and relaxation. It's a time to step away from the hustle and bustle of the working world to trade in business suits for pajamas and to embrace a life of ease. But let's not be too quick to dismiss the significance of what we wear during this phase of our lives. You see, clothing is not merely a fabric; it's a reflection of our identity, our state of mind, and our self-expression. In retirement, the way we dress has a profound impact on our psychological well-being. It can either uplift our spirits, boost our confidence, and add to the joy of each day, or it can subtly erode our self-esteem and leave us feeling unfulfilled.

In this chapter, we'll emphasize the importance of comfort without compromising style. Why, you ask? Retirement is not about letting go of your sense of fashion—it's about evolving it. It's about choosing clothing that suits your lifestyle and makes you feel fantastic. It's about realizing that you don't have to don a business suit to feel empowered; you can be just as confident and stylish in comfortable attire.

New Life, New Wardrobe

Retirement marks the beginning of a new life, and with it comes an opportunity to reinvent not just your daily routine but also your wardrobe. As you step away from your career and embrace a life of leisure, travel, and personal fulfillment, it's essential to align your clothing choices with your retirement lifestyle. Here are the key aspects to consider:

Match Your Clothes to Your Lifestyle

Before diving into your closet and decluttering, take a moment to envision your retirement lifestyle. Are you planning to enjoy the tranquility of a coastal town, explore new cultures through travel, or actively engage in local community activities? Your retirement location and activities should influence your clothing choices. Coastal living may call for casual, breathable fabrics, while a travel-heavy retirement might benefit from versatile, easy-to-pack attire. Consider what's important to you in this new phase of life and let it guide your wardrobe decisions.

Stick to a Budget!

As you revamp your wardrobe, it's important not to get carried away with your budget. While retirement brings freedom and fulfillment, it's also essential to manage your finances thoughtfully. Determine how much you're comfortable spending on your new attire. This budget will help you make informed choices, seek deals, and ensure that your clothing expenditures align with your financial plan. Just because you want to look good doesn't mean you should go broke in the process. Having nice clothes that make you feel confident while still sticking to a budget is possible.

Opportunities for Reinvention

Retirement is an opportunity for reinvention, and your wardrobe is a canvas for self-expression. It's time to redefine your style, explore new trends, and embrace clothing that reflects your evolving identity. If you've always admired a particular fashion aesthetic but couldn't incorporate it into your work attire, now's the time to explore it. Whether it's bohemian chic, classic elegance, or casual comfort, your retirement wardrobe can be a reflection of the real you. The clothing you choose to wear in retirement goes beyond aesthetics; it reflects your lifestyle, priorities, and aspirations. Your wardrobe should enhance your sense of self and empower you to fully embrace this vibrant new chapter in life.

Steps to Streamline Your Wardrobe to Retirement

When it comes to transforming your wardrobe, you can try making use of the clothes that you've always worn, or you can also start with a clean slate. If you're feeling more adventurous and want to build your wardrobe from the ground up, that's great! Streamlining your clothing collection creates space for your new retirement attire and offers a sense of clarity and simplicity to your daily life. Here are the steps to guide you through this process:

1. **Closet Audit**: Begin by conducting a comprehensive closet audit. Take inventory of every piece of clothing you own. Sort them into categories: keep, donate, and discard. Be ruthless in your decision-making, keeping only what you love, what fits well, and what aligns with your retirement lifestyle.

2. **Define Your Style**: Identify your desired style for retirement.

Do you want a wardrobe that's elegant yet comfortable? Are you looking for casual chic or adventure-ready attire? Understanding your preferred style will guide your clothing choices.

3. **Consider Versatility:** Opt for versatile pieces that can be mixed and matched to create different outfits. Versatile items reduce the need for an extensive wardrobe and can be both stylish and functional.

4. **Seasonal Review**: If you're retiring in a location with distinct seasons, assess your clothing to ensure it's appropriate for each. Donate or store items that are not needed for the current season, keeping your closet clutter-free.

5. **Invest in Comfort**: Retirement is all about comfort without sacrificing style. Prioritize comfortable fabrics, well-fitting clothing, and shoes that support your feet while walking, traveling, or pursuing hobbies.

6. **Let Go of the Past**: Part of streamlining your wardrobe is letting go of items tied to your previous career or life phase. It's time to release clothing that no longer serves you and make space for attire that represents the new you.

7. **Create a Capsule Wardrobe:** Consider building a capsule wardrobe—a collection of essential, versatile, and timeless pieces that can be mixed and matched effortlessly. This approach simplifies outfit choices and ensures you have everything you need without excess.

8. **Donations and Discards**: Donate clothing in good condition to

local charities or organizations supporting causes you believe in. Discard items that are beyond use. The act of giving back can be both satisfying and a form of reinvention.

9. **Organize and Accessorize**: Implement an organization system that makes it easy to locate and coordinate your clothing. Invest in quality accessories like scarves, jewelry, or belts that can enhance your outfits without cluttering your closet.

10. **Develop a Shopping Strategy**: Plan your clothing purchases strategically. Focus on quality over quantity and consider shopping for retirement attire seasonally or during sales for added savings.

Fashion To-Dos!

Retirement is a time to enjoy the comfort of everyday living while exuding a sense of style and confidence. Now, if you've always been fashion-forward, then you might be in no need of pointers. However, if you've never really paid attention to how you've dressed before, don't worry. In this section, you will be briefed on the best fashion tips to help you dress appropriately for your age and in the proper context of an event.

Dressing the Part

You can't wear slacks to the gym, and you certainly shouldn't be donning your swim trunks to the dinner table of a family function. Let's go over some of the best fashion practices for every kind of event so that you'll never feel lost or confused about what to do.

Going Out

- For casual outings, opt for well-fitting, quality jeans or comfortable trousers paired with stylish, breathable tops.

- Dress up for special occasions with elegant yet comfortable dresses or dress shirts. Accessories can elevate your look.

Working Out

- Choose moisture-wicking and comfortable athletic wear for workouts. Invest in supportive and stylish athletic shoes.

- Don't forget about fitness-inspired leisure wear—perfect for errands or a post-exercise coffee or brunch date.

Leisure Attire

- Embrace leisurewear that prioritizes comfort without compromising style. Think soft, breathable fabrics and relaxed silhouettes for lounging at home or casual gatherings.

- Invest in versatile pieces like a cozy cardigan or a lightweight, stylish jacket that can be worn for various leisure activities.

Family Events

- Family gatherings call for outfits that strike a balance between casual and polished. Think chinos with a crisp, comfortable shirt or a stylish yet cozy knit sweater.

- Layering can be your friend—add a blazer for a touch of sophistication or a casual jacket for outdoor events.

Travel Clothes

- Choose wrinkle-resistant, versatile pieces that can be mixed and matched for travel. Lightweight, breathable fabrics are essential for comfort during long journeys.

- Don't forget practical accessories like a stylish hat and comfortable, supportive walking shoes for exploration.

- The key to being comfortably stylish in retirement is to invest in clothing that makes you feel good and suits your lifestyle. Prioritize comfort while maintaining your unique sense of style, and you'll be ready to embrace every moment with confidence and grace.

Developing Your Style

Developing a sense of style in retirement is about embracing who you are, understanding your preferences, and curating a wardrobe that reflects your personality and lifestyle. Start by reflecting on your personal style and what makes you feel confident and comfortable. Consider the colors, patterns, and styles that resonate with you. Think about the clothing items that have made you feel your best in the past.

If you're feeling stumped, seek inspiration from various sources. Explore fashion magazines, websites, and social media platforms to discover styles that catch your eye. Look for outfits worn by people whose fashion sense you admire. Also, invest in quality clothing over quantity. Well-made, durable items may cost more upfront, but they last longer and provide better value in the long run. Focus on clothing made from comfortable and breathable materials.

Additionally, don't be afraid to accessorize. Remember that the devil is in the details. Accessories can elevate your style. Consider adding scarves, hats, jewelry, or belts to complete your outfits. They can add a touch of personality and flair to your look. And this should go without saying, but personal grooming is an essential part of style. Keep your hair and grooming routines in line with your fashion choices. Regular grooming ensures you look and feel your best.

Lastly, don't be afraid to experiment with new styles and trends. Style is a reflection of who you are at a given moment, and it can evolve over time. Embrace change and adapt your wardrobe accordingly. Developing your sense of style should be an enjoyable journey. Don't stress over it; have fun and savor the process of curating a wardrobe that makes you feel great.

Sourcing Great Finds

Great. Now, you have a rough idea of what your wardrobe should look like in retirement. Now, the question is, how are you supposed to find the clothes you want to buy? Finding great clothing options involves a combination of knowing where to shop, what to look for, and how to make the most of your shopping experience.

Naturally, you can start by visiting retail stores specializing in clothing for mature individuals. These stores often carry clothing designed with comfort, style, and practicality in mind. Look for brands known for their quality and fit. If you're young, hip, and tech-savvy, you can also use the internet! Online shopping offers a vast selection of clothing options. Explore online retailers that cater to retirees and mature shoppers. Read reviews, check sizing guides, and be sure to understand the return policy before making a purchase.

Don't overlook boutiques and specialty shops, either. These establishments may carry unique and stylish clothing that caters to specific tastes. They can be a great source of one-of-a-kind pieces. Some of these boutiques might even offer pieces that are a better bang for your buck when compared to clothes from global retailers. Thrift and consignment stores can also be treasure troves for retirees. You can find quality clothing at budget-friendly prices. Don't hesitate to explore these options for unique and sustainable choices.

Of course, you should also be mindful of your budget. Keep an eye on sales and discounts, both in physical stores and online. Many retailers offer periodic promotions, making it possible to find stylish clothing at more affordable prices. If you have favorite clothing brands that consistently meet your style and comfort needs, consider sticking with them. Brand loyalty can simplify your shopping experience. And they might even have rewards programs for regular shoppers!

Your Next Steps

Okay. Information overload. Rehauling your entire wardrobe might feel like a Herculean feat, but it doesn't have to be. Let's take it one step at a time. Here are the three tasks that you need to do moving forward when it comes to your wardrobe:

Take the time to make a list of wardrobe pieces that perfectly match your retirement lifestyle. Consider your daily activities, travel plans, and any special occasions you anticipate. Reflect on your personal style preferences. Do you prefer casual comfort, classic elegance, or an eclectic blend? Your intentions list will serve as your fashion roadmap.

Begin your wardrobe transformation by purging items that no longer align with your retirement style intentions. Assess your closet and set aside clothing that doesn't make you feel confident or comfortable. Consider donating or consigning these items for a fresh start. Next, establish a budget for your retirement wardrobe. Decide how much you're comfortable spending and ensure it complements your overall retirement financial plan.

Dive into the world of fashion tips that prioritize both comfort and style. Understand the significance of breathable fabrics, well-fitting clothing, and comfortable footwear. Familiarize yourself with outfit options for various occasions. Know how to strike the right balance between casual and polished for family events or outings. Embrace the importance of developing your unique style and expressing your personality through retirement to break the process of clothing choices.

Chapter Conclusion

For the most part, we've been tackling tasks one at a time, and that's good. The best way to prepare for retirement is to break the process into more manageable bite-sized chunks. Along with other things, retirement is a time for wardrobe reinvention, aligning your clothing choices with your new lifestyle. Creating a budget for your retirement wardrobe is a practical step that ensures your fashion choices complement your financial plan. Remember that opportunities for reinvention are abundant in retirement, allowing you to redefine your style and embrace clothing that reflects the real you.

As you make this stylish transition, remember that retirement is not about letting go of your sense of fashion—it's about evolving it. Your clothing should empower you to enjoy the comfort, confidence, and style you deserve.

In the next chapter, we'll explore the newfound freedom and flexibility that retirement offers. We'll focus on effective daily management and time optimization, helping you maximize your retirement days.

From Rush Hour to Leisurely Hours - Time Management

As we've reiterated over and over again, retirement isn't an endgame. It's an opportunity for reinvention. It's a phase of life where the constraints of a busy career fade away, and you have the gift of time in abundance. But as Taiwanese researchers Wei-Ching Wang, Chang-Yang Wu, and Chung-Chi Wu discovered in their study of 454 retirees, the quality of your retired life isn't solely determined by the hours of free time you possess.

In their study, these researchers found that retirees with more free time weren't necessarily happier than those with less on their schedules. The crucial factor lies in how retirees choose to manage their idle hours. "Individuals who manage their free time well enjoy a higher quality of life, whereas those who gain free time but do not use it properly gain little benefit," the researchers explained (Eisenberg, 2013).

This chapter is about unlocking the secrets of effective time management in retirement. It's about making the most of the leisurely hours that retirement offers, ensuring that each day is a canvas for fulfillment and contentment. Let's explore the art of managing time, seizing opportunities, and crafting a retirement lifestyle that's not just abundant in hours but rich in experiences.

Finally Free!

Retirement is the gateway to a new age of freedom. It's the moment when you shed the work-related responsibilities that have defined your daily life for years. It's a transition from the structured routine that once dictated your schedule to a world where time is now your own. But more significantly, retirement is the grand unveiling of your freedom to do whatever you want.

With retirement, you no longer have to clock in at a specific hour or answer the demands of a boss. Your schedule is now your canvas, and you're the artist who decides how to paint it. The power to shape your day, your week, and your life is in your hands.

However, this newfound freedom, while liberating, can also be overwhelming. It's not uncommon to feel disoriented by the sheer expanse of time suddenly at your disposal. After years of structured routines and busy schedules, you might encounter a peculiar sensation of having too much time on your hands. The clock that once tethered you to meetings, deadlines, and tasks no longer dictates your day. Your workplace, with its rhythm and demands, is now a part of your history. The absence of these familiar rhythms can create a void, leaving you at a crossroads. What do you do with this treasure trove of time?

Set New Goals

Retirement marks a fresh beginning, and setting new goals can infuse purpose and direction into this exciting phase of life. Consider what you've always wanted to achieve but didn't have the time for during your working years. Whether exploring new hobbies, traveling to new destinations, contributing to a cause you're passionate about, or pursuing further education, defining clear objectives provides structure and motivation.

Visualize the life you want in retirement. What experiences, accomplishments, and adventures do you hope to embrace? This vision will serve as the foundation for your goals. Then, divide your retirement goals into smaller, manageable steps. This not only makes them more achievable but also gives you a sense of accomplishment as you progress.

Start a New Routine

Freedom is great, but it can lose its novelty once you run out of things to do. This is where a routine can serve as a comforting and stabilizing force. It doesn't have to mirror your work schedule; it can be tailored to suit your desires. A routine can provide structure, maintain your health and well-being, and ensure you make the most of your time.

You can begin your day with a morning ritual. It might involve exercise, meditation, journaling, or simply a leisurely breakfast. This sets a positive tone for the day. From a weekly perspective, you can set specific objectives to meet. This could include days for physical activity, cultural pursuits, time with loved ones, and personal projects.

Stay Socially Connected

One aspect of retirement that can be disorienting is the shift from a bustling workplace to potentially more solitary days. Social connections are vital for mental and emotional well-being. Make an effort to stay connected with friends, family, and your community. Join clubs or organizations related to your interests. This can lead to new friendships and shared experiences. You might also consider volunteering for a cause that resonates with you. It's a great way to meet like-minded individuals and give back to the community.

Learn New Skills

Retirement offers the perfect opportunity to explore new skills and interests. Whether it's picking up a musical instrument, learning a new language, or taking up a hobby you've always been curious about, acquiring new skills keeps your mind engaged and passionate. The Internet provides many online courses, often for free or at a low cost. This opens up a world of learning possibilities from the comfort of your home.

Balance Isolation and Social Engagement

While social interaction is important, it's also crucial to find a balance that works for you. Some retirees may prefer solitude at times, relishing the peace and quiet of being alone. Allow yourself moments of solitude for reflection, self-care, and relaxation. Use this time to pursue hobbies or simply enjoy your own company. At the same time, stay open to social engagements, whether joining friends for lunch, attending social events, or participating in group activities. Social connections provide companionship and joy. Balancing time for yourself and time for others can be an effective way to make the most out of retirement.

Daily Time Management

Time management is an essential practice, even—and especially—during retirement. You might wonder why you need to manage time when you've bid adieu to structured work hours and commutes. The answer lies in the very essence of time itself. Just because you're not working doesn't mean that you shouldn't be adhering to a schedule anymore. That's the irony of having so much free time. The best way to make the most out of it is to do proper scheduling.

Retirement is a precious gift, and every day is an opportunity to experience life to the fullest. Effective time management ensures you make the most of these valuable moments. By planning your days, you can engage in activities that bring joy, fulfillment, and purpose. A well-managed schedule helps maintain balance, ensures you allocate time to your goals and passions, and provides a sense of order. More than that, it helps you avoid regret. It's a common sentiment to hear retirees express regret over not making the most of their earlier years. Effective time management in retirement helps you avoid similar regrets by making conscious choices about how you spend your days.

That doesn't mean using every second of every day to be productive. The key is not to fill every moment but to use time intentionally. Time management in retirement isn't about rushing from one task to another; it's about savoring each day, maintaining well-being, and pursuing the activities and passions that matter most to you.

How to Manage Your Time Effectively

Time management in retirement doesn't look all that different from time management in one's professional life. However, there is a lot more freedom and mobility in retirement, and the stakes are less high. Nevertheless, here are a few of the best tips that you can practice in order to use your time wisely as a retiree:

Learn How to Prioritize Tasks

Effective time management begins with setting clear priorities. In retirement, you have the freedom to choose how to spend your days, but understanding what matters most to you is essential. Prioritize tasks and activities based on your values, goals, and interests. This ensures you invest your time in what brings you the most fulfillment.

Stick to a Schedule

While retirement offers the luxury of flexibility, a basic schedule can provide a sense of structure. It doesn't need to mimic your former work hours, but it can offer a framework for your day. A schedule helps you allocate time to various activities and ensures you make the most of each moment.

Create a Consistent Exercise Routine

Physical health is a cornerstone of overall well-being. Incorporate regular exercise into your routine. Whether it's daily walks, fitness classes, or any activity that you enjoy, consistency is key. Exercise not only boosts your health but also energizes you for other pursuits.

Spend Time on What You're Passionate About

Retirement is the time to dive into your passions. Identify what truly excites you, whether it's a creative project, a hobby, or a cause you're passionate about. Allocate significant time to these pursuits, and let your passions ignite your days with enthusiasm.

Be Flexible

Flexibility is a hallmark of retirement. It allows you to adapt to the unexpected and seize spontaneous opportunities. While schedules are valuable, they leave room for spontaneity. Being flexible means embracing the joys of unplanned adventures or cherished moments with loved ones.

Don't Multitask

Multitasking can be counterproductive, as it divides your focus and attention. Instead, focus on one task at a time. It allows you to immerse yourself in the moment fully and enhances the quality of your experiences.

Reduce Distractions

Identify common distractions that can hinder your productivity and time management. Whether it's constant email notifications or the lure of social media, minimize these interruptions during your dedicated time for specific tasks.

Find a System That Works

Time management systems can vary from person to person. Experiment with different approaches to discover what works best for you. It might be a digital calendar, a paper planner, or a combination of both. The goal is to find a system that aligns with your preferences and enhances your daily management.

Chapter Conclusion

This chapter taught us that effective time management is about filling your days with tasks, cherishing every moment, and creating a retirement lifestyle that aligns with your passions and aspirations. Ultimately, having more free time doesn't mean that you shouldn't be paying attention to *how* you spend your time. Effective time management is vital for maximizing experiences, maintaining balance, and pursuing your passions.

As you transition into retirement, remember that time is a finite and precious resource. It's a gift to be unwrapped, cherished, and used intentionally. The act of learning how to prioritize, embracing a flexible schedule, nurturing your well-being, and focusing on your passions can make the most out of this chapter of your life.

REDISCOVERING YOUR PASSIONS

*S*urround yourself with what you love, whether it's family, pets, keepsakes, music, plants, hobbies, whatever. –George Carlin

Passion is the heartbeat of a vibrant life. It's the force that makes every day beautiful, meaningful, and interesting. While retirement may be a time of transition and newfound freedom, it's no reason to dim the flames of your passions. In fact, it's an opportunity to stroke them into a brilliant blaze. There's nothing wrong with being passionate, even in retirement, where you're supposedly expected to be relaxing and doing nothing. Our passions are the soul's expression, and they can bring purpose and fulfillment to this remarkable phase of life.

Why Passion Is Important

Passion isn't just a steamy, hot love with a romantic interest. Passion is also manifested in the eyes of a grandchild or in a beautifully written song. It can be manifested in hitting a perfect golf shot or in leveling up in chess.

There are many ways through which passion can manifest itself, especially in retirement. And yet, many people are still deluded into thinking that retirement life is one that's completely devoid of romance, excitement, exhilaration, and passion.

A More Enriching Life

Passion adds depth and richness to your existence. It's the element that transforms everyday activities into extraordinary experiences. In retirement, when you have the freedom to choose how you spend your time, pursuing your passions becomes a means of self-enrichment. It's about immersing yourself in the things that truly matter to you, whether it's art, music, gardening, or any other interest that sets your heart aglow.

Well-Being and Health

Engaging in activities you're passionate about can have profound effects on your well-being and health. The joy and contentment derived from doing what you love can reduce stress and improve mental health. Pursuing physical activities related to your passions can also boost your physical well-being.

Booming Socials

Passion often leads to connections with like-minded individuals. Joining clubs, groups, or communities centered around your interests can be a fantastic way to build new social connections. Socializing and sharing your passions with others can bring immense joy and a sense of belonging.

Personal Growth and Learning

Retirement is a period of personal growth and self-discovery. Pursuing your passions can lead to ongoing self-improvement, skill development, and the exploration of new horizons. It's about continually evolving and embracing the full potential of your abilities. Passion fuels a thirst for knowledge. It encourages lifelong learning and exploration. Whether it's delving into books, taking courses, or simply experimenting with new ideas, your passions can be the guiding light on your journey of continuous discovery.

A Sense of Purpose

Purpose is important for a human being. Our sense of agency and utility relies on having a sense of purpose, and that's something that passion contributes to. Passion gives you a reason to wake up in the morning with enthusiasm and excitement. Retirement can sometimes bring a loss of purpose for those who were deeply committed to their careers. Reigniting old passions or discovering new ones can reignite that sense of direction and fulfillment. It's about living a life that aligns with your true desires, dreams, and values. In retirement, it's about cherishing every moment and embracing a lifestyle that brings you unending joy.

Discovering and Pursuing Your Passions

Passions, particularly in the context of retirement, are the activities, interests, and pursuits that set your heart on fire and fill your soul with unbridled joy. They are the things that make you feel truly alive, content, and inspired. Imagine an activity, interest, or hobby that you want to spend most of your time doing because you genuinely enjoy it. That's likely to be your passion. However, if you're just not the type of person who is interested in anything or has any hobbies beyond your career, that's fine. Let's talk about how you can discover what you're passionate about.

Make a Personal Vision Statement

A personal vision statement is your own unique guide to your aspirations and purpose. It encapsulates what you want to achieve, who you aim to be, and what truly matters to you in retirement. When you create a vision statement, you define your path, focus your energy, and align your actions with your deepest desires.

Define Your Core Values

Your core values are the principles that underpin your decisions, actions, and life choices. Discovering and acknowledging your core values is a crucial step in identifying your passions. They serve as a compass, pointing you toward activities and pursuits that resonate with what you hold most dear.

Determine Your True North

Your *true North* is your authentic self and the life you're meant to lead. It's the compass direction that guides you toward your genuine desires and passions. Navigating toward your true North involves aligning your actions and choices with your innermost beliefs and aspirations.

Create a List of Activities You Enjoy

Your list of joyful activities is essentially a collection of passions waiting to be discovered. Jot down everything, big or small, that brings you happiness. Whether it's reading, dancing, hiking, or simply spending time with loved ones, this list can unveil hidden passions.

Identify the Activities That Don't Resonate With You

Sometimes, uncovering your passions is as much about recognizing what doesn't align with your true desires. Again, time is a finite resource. You shouldn't be spending it on things that don't give you any sense of meaning, purpose, or fulfillment.

Acknowledge Your Strengths and Celebrate Achievements

Recognizing your strengths and celebrating past accomplishments can offer valuable insights into your passions. Your achievements represent areas where you've excelled and found fulfillment. Acknowledging these can point you toward activities that align with your unique abilities and desires.

Try Your Hand at Journaling

Journaling is a powerful tool for self-discovery. It involves regularly writing down your thoughts, feelings, experiences, and aspirations. Journaling provides a space for introspection and can help unveil your passions by offering clarity on what truly matters to you.

Cultivate Mindfulness Through Practice

Mindfulness practice involves being fully present and observing your thoughts and feelings without judgment. It fosters self-awareness, helping you understand your inner desires and interests. Embracing mindfulness can lead to profound discoveries about your passions.

Seek Guidance and Mentorship

Seeking guidance from a coach or mentor can be instrumental in your quest to discover your passions. They can provide expert insights, support, and a structured approach to uncovering hidden talents and interests.

Surround Yourself With Like-Minded Individuals

Building a network of individuals who share your interests and passions can be an inspiring and supportive environment. Being in the company of like-minded people can encourage mutual exploration, spark new interests, and provide a sense of belonging and inspiration.

Making Time for Hobbies

Hobbies are a gateway to discovering and nurturing your passions in retirement. Yes, they are typically seen as pastimes that are designed to keep people occupied. But there's so much more to it than that. In retirement, the concept of a hobby takes on a new depth. It's not just something to fill idle hours; it's a vessel for exploring what truly makes your heart sing. Here's why hobbies and passions are closely intertwined:

Improved Physical and Mental Health

Engaging in hobbies keeps your mind active and your body moving. Whether it's tending to a garden, painting, playing a musical instrument, or any other hobby, these activities promote physical well-being and mental agility. They help you maintain your health, vitality, and zest for life.

Stress Relief

Hobbies serve as a tranquil oasis in the midst of life's demands. They provide a haven where you can escape the stresses of daily life and focus on what you love. This escape not only offers relaxation but also serves as a powerful stress-relief mechanism.

Income Potential

Many retirees discover that their hobbies have the potential to turn into extra income. Whether it's crafting, writing, photography, or any other creative endeavor, you might find that your passion can be shared with others and even generate additional income. This not only adds a financial dimension to your hobbies but also deepens your commitment to your passions.

Embracing hobbies in retirement is about much more than mere recreation; it's about a profound engagement with life.

Great Ideas for Hobbies After Retirement

Unsure about how you're supposed to spend your time? You didn't really have any time for hobbies until now? Don't fret. You're bound to find something that you like. It's just a matter of being brave enough to be adventurous and to expose yourself to different kinds of activities.

Social Hobbies

Social hobbies are activities that encourage interaction and connection with others. They offer the opportunity to forge new friendships and deepen existing ones. Social hobbies are fantastic for staying engaged, sharing experiences, and enhancing your social well-being during retirement.

Examples:

- **Volunteering**: Contribute your time and skills to local nonprofits, community organizations, or charities.

- **Joining a Book Club**: Engage in intellectual discussions with fellow book enthusiasts.

- **Dancing Classes**: Learn to dance, from ballroom to salsa, and enjoy the social atmosphere.

- **Community Gardening**: Collaborate with neighbors to cultivate a community garden.

- **Card Games**: Participate in regular card game sessions with friends and acquaintances.

Outdoor Hobbies

Outdoor hobbies are pursuits that invite you to explore the natural world and enjoy the great outdoors. Whether it's hiking, birdwatching, gardening, cycling, or simply going for a leisurely walk, these hobbies promote physical health, mental rejuvenation, and a profound connection with nature. They can be an excellent way to stay active and relish the beauty of the environment.

Examples:

- **Hiking**: Explore nature and scenic trails in your region or even embark on hiking adventures.

- **Bird-watching:** Invest in binoculars and bird guides to observe local wildlife.

- **Cycling**: Enjoy leisurely bike rides or venture into more challenging routes.

- **Gardening**: Cultivate a beautiful garden filled with flowers, vegetables, or herbs.

- **Photography**: Capture the beauty of the outdoors through photography.

Creative Hobbies

Creative hobbies are outlets for self-expression and imagination. They allow you to explore their artistic side, embrace their passions, and share their unique perspectives with the world. It's a channel for self-discovery and the joy of creation.

Examples:

- **Painting**: Unleash your artistic talent on canvas with acrylics, watercolors, or oils.

- **Writing**: Start a journal, write poetry, or even pen that novel you've always dreamt of.

- **Crafting**: Explore various crafting projects, from knitting to woodworking.

- **Playing an Instrument**: Learn to play a musical instrument like the piano, guitar, or violin.

- **Photography**: Express your creativity through photography, capturing moments and landscapes.

Brain-Boosting Hobbies

Brain-boosting hobbies are activities that stimulate mental agility and enhance cognitive well-being. They keep the mind sharp, foster continuous learning, and provide intellectual satisfaction. Brain-boosting hobbies are essential for maintaining mental fitness in retirement.

Examples:

- **Reading**: Dive into a world of books, from fiction to nonfiction, to stimulate your mind.

- **Crossword Puzzles**: Challenge your vocabulary and problem-solving skills with puzzles.

- **Learning a New Language**:Embark on the journey of mastering a new language or enhancing your existing language skills.

- **Chess or Board Games**: Engage in strategic games like chess, Scrabble, or Settlers of Catan.

- **Educational Courses**: Enroll in online courses or attend local classes to continue learning.

Cultural Hobbies

Each of these categories offers a diverse range of hobbies tailored to retirees' varied interests and preferences. Whether you're drawn to social
connections, outdoor adventures, creative expression, mental challenges,
or cultural exploration, there's a hobby category to ignite your passion in
retirement.

Examples:

- **Museum Visits**: Explore local museums, art galleries, and cultural institutions.

- **Literary Exploration**: Dive into classic and contemporary liter-
ature, attending book readings and literary events.

- **Travel and Cultural Exploration**: Travel to new places, embracing different cultures, traditions, and cuisines.

- **Music and Theater Arts**:Attend classical music concerts, op-
eras, and musical performances.

Chapter Conclusion

That does it for this chapter! We've celebrated the value of passions and
how they add depth, meaning, and beauty to your life, even in retirement.
Even though you might retire from professional life, your passions are not
meant to retire. They are lifelong companions that can light up your days
and infuse them with purpose.

Beyond the sheer joy of pursuing your interests, passions contribute to your overall well-being, offering mental stimulation, emotional fulfillment, and a sense of purpose. Hobbies act as gateways to uncovering passions. They offer a diverse array of experiences and avenues for self-expression. Remember that your passions can guide you through retirement's adventures.

In the next chapter, we'll be exploring grander schemes and adventures that will make up your retirement. We'll discuss the concept of bucket list dreams and how you can spend your time and resources toward achieving them. From adventures across the globe to local discoveries, you'll learn how to dream big and go after what you want.

Living the Bucket List: Travel and Adventures

Traveling tends to magnify all human emotions. –Peter Hoeg

In, it's easy to be swept away by the everyday tasks and responsibilities that often feel like a blur. The mundane routines have their place, but what truly etches its mark on our hearts are the adventures that define our existence. While chores and work may be natural parts of life, the vibrant hues are the journeys and explorations that ignite our spirits.

By embracing a life of exploration and dynamism, you open the door to emotions that reach extraordinary heights and experiences that defy imagination. I can still recall every delicious meal I've eaten, mountains I've hiked, cities I've run through, and travel journals I've written. More than remembering what I was doing, I can still vividly recall how these experiences made me feel.

A Life of Adventure

When you retire, it's comforting to think of you resigning to the safety and solitude of a retirement home. And that's all swell and grand, but you shouldn't limit yourself to believing that that's all you can do. Retirement is also the time to unearth the treasures of the world and, more importantly, the treasures within yourself. The prospect of travel and embarking on adventures can be exhilarating, and it's essential to make it feel reachable and within your grasp, even if it may seem intimidating.

As you step into retirement, consider yourself a free-spirited explorer on the cusp of great discoveries. The world is your playground, waiting for you to leave your footprints in its sands, scale its peaks, and immerse yourself in its cultures. Your bucket list isn't a distant dream; it's a roadmap to the extraordinary. It's a collection of aspirations that are very much within your reach. In retirement, you have the time and freedom to transform these dreams into cherished memories.

The idea of adventure can sometimes be overshadowed by concerns about practicalities, logistics, and financial constraints. And it's okay to have those concerns. After all, travel can be quite intimidating. But you shouldn't let that turn you off to the idea of seeing the world in all its glory. In this chapter, we'll break down these barriers, providing insights on how to make your adventures feasible and affordable.

Practical Advice for Planning Trips

Embarking on an adventure is an exhilarating prospect, but to ensure your travels go smoothly, practical planning is essential. Here, we'll provide you with valuable tips on planning your trips, making your adventures not just reachable but truly enjoyable. And don't worry; we'll cover all the bases, from researching destinations right down to learning how to pack properly.

Destinations

Start by researching destinations that align with your interests. Whether exploring historical cities, relaxing on pristine beaches, or venturing into the heart of nature, choose destinations that resonate with your passions.

Travel Documents

Start by checking the validity of your passport and any required visas. If your passport is nearing its expiration date, renew it in advance. Verify whether your chosen destinations have specific entry requirements, such as visas or travel insurance, and ensure all documents are.

Peak Seasons

Understanding peak and off-peak travel seasons is crucial. Traveling during off-peak times can result in reduced costs, fewer crowds, and a more relaxed experience. Be aware of local holidays and festivals that may impact your travel.

Activities and Sights

Investigate the attractions, activities, and sights available at your chosen destination. Create a list of "must-see" places and experiences. This ensures you make the most of your visit and don't miss out on iconic landmarks or unique local experiences.

Accommodations and Meals

Selecting suitable accommodation and dining options is vital for a comfortable trip. Research different types of lodgings, from hotels to Airbnb, and choose the ones that align with your budget and preferences. Explore local dining options to savor the regional cuisine and immerse yourself in the culture.

Transportation Options

Consider the best transportation methods for your destination. Depending on the location, you might choose to rent a car for flexibility, rely on public transportation for affordability, or opt for guided tours for an in-depth experience. Research transportation options to plan your itinerary effectively.

Advanced Reservations

To minimize last-minute stress and secure your preferred choices, make reservations in advance. This includes booking accommodations, tours, and activities. Reservations ensure you have a spot and can help you take advantage of early booking discounts.

Packing Your Bag

Efficient packing is essential for a comfortable journey. Make a checklist of essentials based on the duration and nature of your trip. Go for versatile clothing items that can be mixed and matched. Consider the weather conditions at your destination and pack accordingly. Don't forget to bring any necessary medications, travel adaptors, and specific items related to your chosen activities.

How to Create a Bucket List

A bucket list is a collection of aspirations and experiences you wish to accomplish during your lifetime. It's essentially a catalog of dreams, both big and small that you hope to achieve before you "kick the bucket"—a colloquial phrase that inspired the term. Many people will use their retirement as an opportunity to check items off their bucket lists with all their extra time and resources.

Creating a bucket list is an act of self-discovery, a way to crystallize your desires and infuse your life with purpose. In retirement, your bucket list can serve as your new fixation. It can be what you devote your energy and time to. A bucket list is a testament to your unique journey, showcasing the adventures you wish to undertake and the memories you plan to create.

Here's how you can go about creating your bucket list:

Reflect on Your Passions and Interests

- What activities, experiences, or places have always intrigued you?

- Consider your hobbies, interests, and things you've always wanted to learn or try.

- Reflect on the moments in life when you felt the most alive and fulfilled. What were you doing?

Think About Your Dreams and Goals

- What are your long-held dreams or aspirations for your retirement years?

- What personal or professional goals have you yet to achieve?

- Are there any regrets or unfulfilled wishes you'd like to address?

Consider Your Travel Preferences

- Where in the world have you always wanted to visit? What specific destinations hold a special place in your heart?

- Are you drawn to cultural experiences, natural wonders, adventurous activities, or relaxation on pristine beaches?

- Do you prefer solo travel, family adventures, or group tours?

Additional Tips

- **Break Your List Down Into Categories**: Organize your bucket list into categories, such as travel, personal growth, fitness, and relationships. This helps you create a well-rounded list that reflects all aspects of your life.

- **Set Achievable Goals**: Ensure that your bucket list contains a mix of both short-term and long-term goals. Some experiences can be accomplished in a weekend, while others may require more time and planning.

- **Embrace New Experiences**: Challenge yourself to include items that push you out of your comfort zone. Try new foods, activities, and cultures that you haven't explored before.

- **Prioritize and Organize**: Determine which experiences matter most to you and prioritize your list accordingly. Organize your list by setting timelines and milestones for each goal.

Getting From Dream to Reality

Vision without action is merely a dream. –Joel A. Barker

Writing dreams onto your bucket list doesn't mean you're guaranteed to achieve them. You have to put forth the effort to turn those dreams into a reality, but that's easier said than done. That's why you need to do proper planning and time management for you to make sure that your wishes eventually manifest in real life. In order to achieve your goals, you need to take a holistic approach to breaking them down and determining your game plan moving forward. To do this, you need to take a look at various aspects of your life and see how they all contribute to your goals. This can differ from person to person, but for the most part, these are the facets of life that you need to look into:

1. Physical

2. Financial

3. Emotional/Spiritual

4. Relationships

5. Time

6. Logistical

When you set a goal on your bucket list, try to reflect on what habits you can incorporate for each of these facets to contribute to your overall goal. For example, let's say that you set a bucket list to do the Camino de

Santiago pilgrimage. This is how you should approach that larger goal with mini goals:

1. **Physical**: Prepare your body for the physical demands of the pilgrimage. Establish a consistent exercise routine that includes walking and hiking. Gradually increase the distance and difficulty of your walks.

2. **Financial**: Ensure you have the necessary funds for the pilgrimage. Create a dedicated savings account for your pilgrimage. Develop a monthly budget to allocate funds toward this goal.

3. **Emotional/Spiritual**: Prepare your mind and spirit for the transformative experience. Dedicate time each day for mindfulness practices like meditation, journaling, or spiritual reflection.

4. **Relationship**: Keep your loved ones informed and engaged in your journey. Regularly communicate with family and friends to share your plans, reassure them about your safety, and keep them involved in your experience.

5. **Time**: Efficiently plan and manage your time leading up to the pilgrimage. Use a calendar or planner to schedule your training, budgeting, and preparation tasks. Set deadlines for each step.

6. **Logistical**: Ensure all logistical details are sorted before departure. Research the Camino de Santiago, including routes, accommodations, and necessary gear. Create a detailed itinerary, make reservations, and obtain the required permits or documents.

Fulfilling a bucket list item isn't always going to be an easy feat. Your loftiest goals will require a holistic approach encompassing physical preparation, financial discipline, emotional and spiritual readiness, relationships, effective time management, and meticulous logistical planning. While difficult, it's not impossible; you can break the larger dream down into simpler goals and habits.

Bucket List Ideas for Retirement

The beauty of the bucket list is that it can be filled with absolutely anything you want. And while you might feel the pressure to overload your list with just about everything, try to restrain yourself. Choose activities or goals you know resonate with you and would find fulfillment in. If you're stumped and you don't know where to start, here are a few ideas that you might be able to borrow from:

Travel Experiences

- Walk the Camino de Santiago pilgrimage.

- Explore the Amazon Rainforest.

- Cruise the Norwegian Fjords.

- Visit iconic cities like Paris, Rome, and Tokyo.

- Take a road trip along Route 66.

- Go on a wildlife safari in Africa.

- Discover the wonders of the Galápagos Islands.

- Experience the Northern Lights in Scandinavia.

Cultural Experiences

- Attend the Carnival in Rio de Janeiro.

- Witness the sunrise at Machu Picchu.

- Learn a new language.

- Take cooking classes in Tuscany.

- Attend a traditional Japanese tea ceremony.

- Experience a live opera or ballet performance.

- Volunteer at a local cultural festival.

Personal Development

- Earn a degree or certificate in a subject of interest.

- Write and publish a book or memoir.

- Complete a challenging hiking trail, like the Appalachian Trail.

- Participate in a mindfulness or meditation retreat.

- Take up a new artistic hobby, like painting or photography.

- Learn to play a musical instrument.

Family and Relationships

- Plan a family reunion in a picturesque location.

- Organize a surprise party for a loved one.

- Write heartfelt letters to family members and friends.

- Foster a rescue pet or volunteer at an animal shelter.

- Reconnect with old friends or long-lost relatives.

- Create a family tree and document your family history.

Health and Wellness

- Train for and complete a marathon or triathlon.

- Commit to a regular fitness regimen.

- Achieve and maintain a healthy weight.

- Try yoga, Pilates, or tai chi.

- Embrace a plant-based diet.

- Explore holistic and alternative therapies.

Charitable Experiences

- Donate to a charitable cause or establish your own.

- Organize a charity event or fundraiser.

- Mentor a young person or offer life guidance.

- Volunteer at a homeless shelter or food bank.

Chapter Conclusion

Retirement gives you the time and resources to pursue things you were never able to do throughout your working life. From embarking on epic journeys to embracing cultural wonders, we've delved into the joy of creating experiences that will add a sense of meaning and fulfillment to your life. Bucket lists are deeply personal catalogs of your dreams and aspirations. While they can be intimidating, there's no better time to pursue these dreams than retirement. Break down your grand adventures into manageable mini goals across various facets of life. And always value the process of getting to where you want to go. The journey to fulfilling your bucket list is as important as the destination itself.

In the next chapter, we'll broach the topic of choosing the proper living arrangements for you in retirement. You would be surprised at the tremendous impact community involvement can have on your newfound sense of purpose. The adventure continues in every corner of your life, and your retirement journey is far from over.

Retirement Communities - Building New Social Networks

M aking friends as an adult can be a daunting endeavor, which has to do with the multifaceted nature of adulthood itself. Unlike childhood and adolescence, where school and shared experiences often facilitate friendships, adults are spread across diverse life stages, work environments, and personal responsibilities. It's no wonder that many find it challenging to build new social networks in their retirement years.

While the reasons can be complex and varied, several factors contribute to the difficulty adults face when forming new connections. Unlike school or college, where social interaction is inherent, adults often have fewer built-in opportunities to meet and connect with others. Aside from that, the demands of careers, family, and daily life can leave little time for socializing.

As people age, they may generally become more resistant to change, including opening up to new friendships. Adults can be more cautious about putting themselves out there, fearing rejection or awkward encounters. This guardedness and the diversity of life can make finding common interests and shared experiences more challenging.

However, the beauty of retirement is that it presents a unique opportunity to address these challenges. One of the key elements in this quest for new friendships is choosing the right living arrangement and community involvement. This chapter will touch on the various options available and provide you with valuable insights on creating meaningful connections in your retirement years.

Living Arrangements

As you approach retirement, you'll find that your living arrangements play a pivotal role in shaping your daily life and social experiences. Whether you're considering downsizing, exploring independent living, or pondering the potential of retirement communities, each choice holds unique benefits and considerations. It's important that you are aware of all your options and make an informed decision on how to proceed with this next phase of your life.

Downsizing

Simplify Your Space and Enrich Your Lifestyle

The concept of downsizing is a liberating and often transformative choice that many retirees embrace. It's about decluttering your physical space to simplify your life, reduce maintenance demands, and open the door to new opportunities. It's more than just a reduction of square footage; it's a mindful choice to simplify your living situation and embrace a lifestyle that aligns with your retirement goals.

Less Financial Strain and Oversight

A smaller home typically lowers mortgage or rent payments, reduces property taxes, and decreases utility costs. This newfound financial freedom can be channeled into your retirement savings, travel, or pursuing hobbies and experiences. On top of that, a smaller living space translates to fewer maintenance tasks, which means less time spent on chores like cleaning, yard work, and home repairs. This newfound free time can be devoted to social activities, travel, or personal interests.

Enhanced Flexibility and Social Opportunities

Downsizing offers the flexibility to choose a location that aligns with your lifestyle preferences. Whether it's a vibrant urban setting, serene countryside, or a coastal retreat, you can tailor your living arrangements to your ideal retirement destination. Smaller homes are often single-level or equipped with accessibility features, making it easier to age in place. This means you can enjoy your home for longer, maintaining your independence and quality of life.

Downsizing also often leads to living in communities where you're in closer proximity to your neighbors. This proximity encourages spontaneous social interactions and creates an environment where it's easier to form connections and friendships.

Better Peace of Mind

Lastly, downsizing necessitates decluttering and simplifying your belongings. This process can be cathartic, allowing you to let go of possessions that no longer serve you and focus on what truly matters. Many retirees find that a smaller, cozier living space fosters a sense of comfort and contentment. It's easier to create an environment that reflects your personality and interests, enhancing your emotional well-being.

What Is Independent Living?

Independent living is a living arrangement designed for active and self-reliant seniors who want to maintain their autonomy, live comfortably, and enjoy a socially engaging lifestyle without the burdens of homeownership or the responsibilities of daily maintenance. This retirement housing option provides a balance between personal freedom and community support.

Independent living typically involves residing in specialized retirement communities, apartment complexes, or housing facilities specifically designed for seniors. These communities offer a range of housing options, from apartments to freestanding cottages, each equipped with features that cater to senior needs, such as grab bars and wheelchair accessibility.

Independent living arrangements can come in different shapes and forms:

Retirement Communities

Retirement communities are planned residential developments specifically designed for active seniors. They offer housing options, including single-family homes, townhouses, and apartments. These communities often provide amenities like fitness centers, social activities, and maintenance services.

Congregate Care

Congregate care is a housing option that combines independent living with certain support services like meals, housekeeping, and transportation. Residents in congregate care facilities have their own living spaces but can access these services on-site.

Active Adult

Active adult communities are typically age-restricted neighborhoods designed for individuals aged 55 and older. They offer a range of amenities and activities, catering to the active and independent lifestyle of seniors who desire a sense of community.

Senior-Living Apartments

Senior living apartments are apartment complexes or buildings specifically designed for older adults. These apartments often feature age-friendly amenities and services, making them a comfortable and convenient choice for independent living.

Continuing Care Retirement Community

Continuing Care Retirement Communities (CCRCs) are comprehensive retirement communities that offer a continuum of care, from independent living to assisted living and skilled nursing care. This arrangement allows residents to age in place, knowing they have a range of services as their needs change.

Senior Cohousing

Senior cohousing is a unique concept where older adults live in a community where they have their own private homes but share communal spaces and responsibilities. This arrangement promotes a strong sense of community and support among residents.

Is It Right for You?

Determining if independent living is the right choice for your retirement lifestyle involves considering several key factors. And this is certainly not a decision that you should take lightly. Here are some essential questions to help you assess whether independent living aligns with your needs and preferences:

- **Are You Looking for an Active Social Life?** Independent living communities emphasize social engagement. If you're eager to participate in group activities, make new friends, and enjoy a vibrant social life, this option may be suitable for you.

- **Do You Desire a Maintenance-Free Lifestyle?** Independent living frees you from many household maintenance tasks. If you'd prefer to have more leisure time and less property upkeep, this type of arrangement can be attractive.

- **Are You Ready to Downsize?** Downsizing is often part of the independent living transition. If you're open to reducing your living space and decluttering your belongings, you may find this option appealing.

- **Do You Want Access to Amenities and Services?** Independent living communities offer a variety of amenities and services, from dining options to fitness centers. If you value easy access to such conveniences, independent living could be a good fit.

- **Is Flexibility Important to You?** Independent living arrangements often offer flexibility in the services and amenities you can choose. If you prefer a customized approach to your retirement living, this flexibility can be advantageous.

- **Do You Value Safety and Security?** Many independent living communities prioritize the safety and security of their residents. If this is a top concern for you, these communities often offer secure entry systems and 24/7 emergency response.

- **Are You Interested in an Age-Appropriate Environment?** Independent living communities are typically designed with senior-friendly features. If you appreciate living in an environment tailored to your age group's needs, this arrangement may suit you.

- **Are You Comfortable With a Monthly Fee?** Independent living often involves a monthly fee for services and amenities. Consider whether you're comfortable with this financial arrangement and whether it fits within your retirement budget.

- **Do You Want to Retain Your Independence?** Independent living is designed for active and self-reliant seniors who want to maintain autonomy. If you value your independence and the ability to make your own decisions, this option supports that lifestyle.

- **Is the Location Appealing to You?** The location of the independent living community matters. Consider whether the setting aligns with your preferences and lifestyle choices.

Take some time to ponder these questions. Consult your loved ones on what they think. Again, this is not a decision that you want to take lightly. After all, your future living arrangements can impact your quality of life moving forward. Remember that this decision is a highly personal one and should be tailored to your unique aspirations and needs.

Myths About Independent Living

The decision to transition to independent living is personal and often influenced by individual preferences, needs, and lifestyle goals. However, this choice may have its fair share of myths and misconceptions. These stigmas can create doubts and misunderstandings about what independent living entails. It's important that we debunk these misconceptions so that you always make well-informed decisions about your future.

- **It's the Same as a Nursing Home**: One of the most common misconceptions is that independent living is the same as a nursing home. In reality, independent living is designed for active seniors who can live independently and make their own choices. It's far from the clinical environment of a nursing home.

- **It's Expensive**: While there are costs associated with indepen-

dent living, it doesn't necessarily mean it's prohibitively expensive.
Many communities offer a range of pricing options to suit various
budgets, and the cost often includes amenities and services that
can be cost-effective in the long run.

- **It's Only for the Elderly**: Independent living communities cater
  to a diverse group of seniors, and there is no strict age limit. Many
  residents are in their 60s, 70s, and beyond, but some are younger
  retirees who choose this lifestyle for its social opportunities and
  convenience.

- **Loss of Independence**: Some individuals fear that moving to an
  independent living community means surrendering their independence. On the contrary, these communities are designed to
  enhance residents' independence by freeing them from certain
  household chores and responsibilities.

- **It's Boring**: Many believe that retirement communities are dull
  and lacking in excitement. In truth, independent living communities offer a wide range of activities and social opportunities to
  keep residents engaged and entertained.

- **You'll Lose Connection With the Outside World**: Independent living communities actually promote residents' connections
  with the broader community. They often provide transportation
  services, allowing residents to explore the surrounding area and
  maintain ties with friends and family.

- **It's Only for Individuals With Health Issues**: Independent
  living is not exclusively for those with health issues or mobility

concerns. It is suitable for active, healthy seniors who want to enjoy their retirement years in a community setting.

- **You'll Have to Give Up Your Current Lifestyle**: Transitioning to independent living doesn't necessarily mean giving up your current lifestyle. It's about adapting your living situation to better align with your retirement goals and preferences.

- **It's Only for Those Without Family Support**: Independent living can be an attractive option for individuals with strong family support, as well as those without close family ties. The choice to transition to this living arrangement is a personal one, and it can provide valuable social connections and convenience.

At the end of the day, you should always know what you're getting yourself into. Planning for your future necessitates a high level of awareness of all the variables of any decision you make. And that includes knowing whether something is a myth or misconception.

How to Choose the Right Retirement Home

Selecting the right retirement home involves a thorough evaluation of various factors to ensure that the community aligns with your unique lifestyle and preferences. The best choice for one person may not necessarily work for others. Remember that we are all unique and have our own individual goals, interests, and experiences. Your decision on a retirement home is a personal one, and it's important that you look at it from multiple angles. Here are some of the key aspects to consider:

- **Dining Options**: Assess the dining services provided. Do they offer flexible meal plans and a variety of menu options to accommodate your dietary preferences and needs?

- **Community Atmosphere**: Explore the social environment of the community. Do you feel a sense of camaraderie and connection among residents, and does it reflect your ideal social setting?

- **On-Site Services**: Examine the availability of essential services like housekeeping, maintenance, laundry, and personal care assistance, which can enhance your daily living experience.

- **Amenities**: Consider the amenities offered, such as fitness centers, swimming pools, recreational facilities, and common areas for gatherings and events.

- **Wellness Programs**: Look into wellness programs and fitness activities. Does the community provide exercise classes, health services, and programs to promote your overall well-being?

- **Pet Policies**: If you're a pet owner, understand the community's pet policies and whether they allow you to bring your beloved companion with you.

- **Transportation** Services: Evaluate transportation options. Is there convenient access to transportation for shopping, medical appointments, and local outings?

- **Emergency Medical Services**: Inquire about the availability of emergency medical services or the proximity of healthcare facilities to ensure prompt access to medical care when needed.

- **Activities and Hobbies**: Explore the variety of activities and hobbies available. Does the community offer engaging programs that align with your interests and passions?

- **Cost Structure**: Understand the cost structure and financial commitments involved in residing in the retirement home. Are there flexible payment options and a transparent fee schedule?

- **Location**: Consider the location and its proximity to family, friends, and essential amenities such as healthcare providers, shopping centers, and recreational opportunities.

- **Safety and Security**: Investigate safety and security measures in place to ensure you feel secure and protected in your new home.

- **Size and Layout**: Examine the size and layout of living spaces. Ensure that your accommodation meets your space and layout preferences.

The manner in which you prioritize these different variables is up to you. Some people might prefer to err on the side of a place with overly stocked emergency services, while others might prioritize a large living space. It's all a matter of priority and preference. There's no right or wrong here. You have to make the best decision for yourself.

How to Make Friends After You Retire

For many older adults, the prospect of making new friends in retirement can initially seem daunting. The natural progression of life often means that established social circles might have diminished with time, and the opportunity to form new connections may feel limited. However, it's essential to recognize that this doesn't have to be the case. With the right mindset and some proactive steps, you can create meaningful connections with like-minded individuals. Here are some tips to help you make friends after retirement:

- **Join Clubs and Groups:** Seek out clubs, hobby groups, or organizations that align with your interests. Whether it's a book club, a hiking group, or a charitable organization, shared activities provide an excellent platform for forming connections.

- **Volunteer**: Volunteering not only allows you to give back to the community but also provides opportunities to meet others who share your values and passions.

- **Participate in Community Activities**: Engage in local community events, workshops, or classes. These gatherings are excellent places to meet neighbors and fellow retirees.

- **Attend Social Gatherings:** Don't decline invitations to social events or get-togethers. Participate in community gatherings and celebrations, even if it's out of your comfort zone.

- **Embrace Technology**: Use social media and online platforms to stay in touch with family and friends and connect with others who share your interests. Many retirees find online communities to be valuable sources of friendship.

- **Be Open and Approachable**: Maintain an open and approachable demeanor. Smile, make eye contact, and be willing to strike up conversations with people you encounter in your daily life.

- **Take Classes**: Enroll in classes or workshops that interest you, whether it's a cooking class, art course, or language lesson. These environments foster learning and socializing.

- **Host Gatherings**:Don't hesitate to host gatherings or events at your home. This offers a warm and inviting setting for neighbors and acquaintances to connect.

Making friends is all just a matter of giving yourself the right opportunities. It's a rewarding journey that can enhance your overall well-being and enrich your life with new experiences.

Chapter Conclusion

While it's natural to feel apprehensive about making new friends later in life, we've learned that retirement is a golden opportunity for fostering fresh relationships and cherishing existing ones. It's always possible to forge meaningful connections in your retirement years.

From joining clubs and volunteering to embracing the digital age and being open to new experiences, we've learned different approaches to c enriching social connections. With the right mindset and a dash of proactive spirit, you can have a vibrant social life that enhances your retirement journey.

In the next chapter, we'll have to shift gears and talk about more serious matters, particularly in the context of your financial well-being. The goal is to help you gain a comprehensive understanding of your financial situation and provide guidance on setting and achieving retirement goals. Whether you're considering your retirement savings or planning exciting adventures, we'll navigate the financial landscape together, ensuring that your retirement is as fulfilling and financially secure as you've envisioned.

Financial Freedom - Planning for Retirement Bliss

P lanning for your financial well-being in retirement is not just a prudent decision; it's the key to unlocking a future filled with contentment, security, and endless possibilities. While it may be *taboo* for some to talk about money so openly and candidly, it's important that you are empowered enough to have a comprehensive understanding of your financial standing. This will give you the valuable insights that you need to achieve your retirement goals.

Financial freedom is not about accumulating vast wealth; it's about having the resources and strategies in place to lead the retirement life you desire. This chapter will help you take control of your finances and pave the way for a secure retirement where you can embrace your dreams with confidence. The fact of the matter for many is that retirement can be scary, especially when it comes to thinking about finances. That's why you want to practice diligence as early as now in order to ensure that your future self is free from any worries.

Understanding Your Current Financial Situation

Your journey to financial freedom begins with self-awareness, which is the key to charting a course tailored to your unique goals and circumstances, particularly during retirement. And don't worry if you don't have any financial background. This section, along with the other sections of this chapter, will take a very easy and simplified approach to understanding personal finance. All you really need to secure your financial freedom is knowledge of the basics. From there, it's a matter of practicing diligence and discipline by making sure that your finances are always on track.

What Is a Personal Financial Statement?

A Personal Financial Statement, often referred to as a PFS, is a comprehensive document that offers a holistic view of your financial situation. It serves as a financial "snapshot" and includes all the relevant details about your assets, liabilities, income, and expenses. Don't worry; we'll be breaking all of these individual variables down later on. Essentially, this document helps you gauge your current financial health, identify areas for improvement, and plan for your retirement goals effectively.

A Personal Financial Statement offers retirees an accurate depiction of their financial standing, enabling them to make informed decisions about retirement planning, budgeting, and investment strategies. It's an essential tool to understand where you currently stand and plot a course toward a more secure and fulfilling retirement.

Assessing Assets and Liabilities

Assets encompass everything you own that holds monetary value and can contribute to your overall financial worth. Here are examples of assets that you might have:

- **Cash**: The money you have in checking or savings accounts.

- **Savings and Investments**: These encompass savings accounts, certificates of deposit (CDs), stocks, bonds, and mutual funds.

- **Real Estate:** Any property or land you own, such as your home or investment properties.

- **Retirement Accounts**: Your 401(k), IRA, or other retirement savings.

- **Personal Property**: Valuables like jewelry, art, or antiques.

- **Real Estate:**Investment properties, farmland, or commercial properties.

- **Vehicles**: Cars, boats, and other forms of transportation.

- **Business Interests:** If you have ownership in a business or partnerships.

- **Valuable Personal Assets**: Collectibles, vintage cars, or rare items.

On the other hand, liabilities represent your financial obligations or debts. These are some common examples of liabilities:

- **Credit Card Debt**: The balances you owe on your credit cards.

- **Short-Term Loans**: Personal loans or lines of credit.

- **Utility Bills**: Outstanding bills for electricity, water, and gas.

- **Taxes Payable**: Any taxes you owe to the government.

- **Mortgages**: Loans for real estate, like your home.

- **Student Loans**: Education loans that may take years to repay.

- **Car Loans:** Loans used to purchase vehicles.

- **Long-Term Personal Loans**: Loans with a repayment term extending beyond a year.

Your assets and liabilities are tied into calculating your net worth (which we'll discuss later). Essentially, understanding your assets and liabilities gives you a big-picture perspective of your current financial situation.

Income vs. Expenses

You probably already have a good understanding of the difference between income and expenses. But let's try to explore this subject a little deeper. The financial balance of your life can be defined by the relationship between your income and expenses. Income refers to the money you earn or receive on a regular basis. In the context of retirement, there are various sources of income:

- **Employment Income**: This is your salary or wages if you continue to work during retirement. Some retirees opt for part-time jobs, consulting, or freelance work to supplement their retirement income.

- **Social Security Benefits**:A government program providing financial support to retirees. The amount you receive depends on your earnings history and the age at which you begin claiming benefits.

- **Pension Payments**: If you have a pension plan through your employer, you may receive monthly pension payments in retirement.

- **Retirement Account Distributions**: This includes withdrawals from retirement accounts like 401(k)s and IRAs, which may be subject to taxes.

- **Investment Income**: Earnings from investments such as dividends from stocks, interest from bonds, and rental income from real estate.

- **Annuities**: Periodic payments from annuity contracts that you purchased before retirement.

- **Rental Income**: If you own investment properties, the rental income you receive can be a source of income.

- **Part-Time Work**: Many retirees choose to work part-time to supplement their income and stay active.

Expenses are the financial obligations and costs you incur in your daily life. In retirement, understanding and managing your expenses is crucial. Here are the types of expenses you may encounter:

- **Housing Expenses**:This includes mortgage or rent payments, property taxes, insurance, utilities, and maintenance costs.

- **Healthcare Expenses**: Healthcare can be a significant expense in retirement, covering health insurance, medical bills, and prescription medications.

- **Transportation Expenses**: Costs associated with owning and maintaining vehicles, such as fuel, insurance, maintenance, and public transportation.

- **Food and Groceries**:Expenses for groceries, dining out, and entertainment.

- **Debt Payments**:If you have any outstanding debts, such as credit card balances, personal loans, or mortgages, you must consider the corresponding payments.

- **Entertainment and Leisure**: Costs associated with hobbies, travel, dining out, and entertainment.

- **Insurance Premiums**: Payments for various insurance policies, including health, life, auto, and home insurance.

- **Taxes**: This includes income taxes, property taxes, and sales taxes.

- **Utilities**: Regular bills for electricity, gas, water, and other utilities.

- **Charitable Giving**: Contributions to charitable organizations or causes you support.

- **Miscellaneous Expenses**: This category includes a wide range of miscellaneous costs, such as personal care, home improvements, and other discretionary spending.

Balancing your income and expenses is a critical aspect of financial planning for retirement. It's essential to maintain a budget that aligns with your financial goals and ensures your retirement funds are sufficient to cover your desired lifestyle and expenses. Here's how you can do it:

1. Start by creating a detailed budget that outlines your sources of income and various expense categories. Use budgeting software, spreadsheets, or even pen and paper to keep track of your finances.

2. List all your income sources, including employment income, Social Security benefits, pension payments, retirement account distributions, investment income, and any other sources of funds. Be sure to include the amounts and frequency of each income stream.

3. Categorize your expenses into specific categories like housing, healthcare, transportation, food, debt payments, entertainment, and more. This helps you gain a comprehensive view of your spending habits.

4. Make it a habit to record your expenses daily or weekly. Use receipts, bank statements, or financial apps to track each expense accurately. Be meticulous in recording even small expenses.

5. Consider using budgeting apps or software that can automatically categorize and track your expenses, providing you with insights into your financial habits. Popular tools include Mint, YNAB (You Need a Budget), and Quicken. If you're more old-school and prefer to track your budget manually, that's fine, too. Periodically review your budget to see how closely your actual income and expenses align with your budgeted amounts. This practice can

help you identify areas where you may need to cut back or allocate more resources.

6. Establish clear financial goals for your retirement, such as building an emergency fund, paying off debts, or saving for specific retirement dreams. Your budget should reflect these objectives.

7. If you experience significant income changes or life events, such as moving or healthcare costs, be prepared to adjust your budget accordingly.

8. Ensure that your budget includes savings for retirement, emergencies, and other financial goals. Make saving a nonnegotiable part of your budget.

What's that old cliché? If you fail to plan, you plan to fail. Tracking your income and expenses is a crucial aspect of your financial planning. It empowers you to make informed financial decisions, live within your means, and work toward your retirement goals.

Net Worth Calculation

Net worth is a financial metric that provides an overall view of your financial health. It represents the difference between your total assets and your total liabilities. It's the value of everything you own (assets) minus everything you owe (liabilities). Net worth is a significant indicator of your financial well-being and can be a powerful tool for tracking your progress toward financial goals, including retirement planning.

Whether you're considering major purchases, investments, or debt management, understanding your net worth can guide your financial decisions.

It informs you whether you can afford specific expenses or whether it's time to reduce debt or increase savings.

Here's how you can calculate your net worth:

Formula:

1. Create a comprehensive list of all your assets. These may include savings accounts, investments, retirement accounts, real estate, vehicles, jewelry, and other valuables.

2. Assign a fair market value to each asset. For liquid assets like savings accounts or investments, this is straightforward. For physical assets like real estate or vehicles, you may need professional appraisals or online valuation tools.

3. Make a list of all your liabilities, such as mortgages, auto loans, credit card debt, student loans, and any other outstanding loans or financial obligations.

4. Add up the values of all your assets.

5. Add up the balances of all your liabilities.

6. Subtract your total liabilities from your total assets. The result is your net worth.

A positive net worth means your assets exceed your liabilities, indicating financial health. A negative net worth implies that your debts outweigh your assets, suggesting that you may need to focus on debt reduction and financial planning.

Setting Retirement Goals

We've already talked about setting goals for experiences and travel, but it's also important that you learn how to set goals for your finances. Retirement goals are the financial objectives and targets you set for your post-work life. They are essential for ensuring financial security and achieving the retirement lifestyle you desire. These goals can include factors like retirement age, the level of income you want in retirement, and the resources you'll need to maintain your chosen standard of living.

Determining your retirement needs is a critical step in setting retirement goals. This involves evaluating a number of various factors, such as:

- **Lifestyle Expectations**: Consider your desired retirement lifestyle, including housing, travel, hobbies, and other expenses.

- **Inflation**: Account for the impact of inflation on the cost of living over time.

- **Healthcare Costs**: Recognize the potential costs of healthcare and medical expenses in retirement.

- **Expected Lifespan**: Estimate how long you'll need to support your retirement lifestyle.

- **Other Financial Obligations**: Include any outstanding debts or financial responsibilities.

Now, there is no fixed method to setting your financial goals for retirement, but there are some key steps that you want to make sure are covered:

- **Start Simple**: Begin by setting straightforward and achievable retirement goals. For example, aim to save a specific amount of money each month or increase your retirement account contributions gradually.

- **Determine How Much You Can Put Toward Retirement**: Analyze your current financial situation and assess how much you can comfortably allocate to retirement savings. This should be a budget-friendly amount that doesn't strain your current lifestyle.

- **Understand How Much Time You Have to Save for Retirement**: The sooner you start saving for retirement, the more time your investments have to grow. Understanding your timeline is crucial for setting realistic goals.

- **Understand Your Spending Needs**: Evaluate your current spending patterns and estimate how they might change in retirement. Consider factors like downsizing, healthcare costs, and lifestyle choices.

- **Investing for the Long Term**: Develop a well-thought-out investment strategy that aligns with your retirement goals. Diversify your portfolio to manage risk while seeking returns that outpace inflation.

- **Adjust When Necessary**:Be flexible in adjusting your retirement goals as your financial situation evolves. Life changes, such as career shifts, windfalls, or unexpected expenses, may impact your ability to save for retirement. Regularly review and adapt your goals to stay on track.

- **Professional Advice**:Consider consulting a financial advisor or retirement specialist. They can provide valuable guidance, conduct retirement projections, and help you set realistic and achievable goals.

Setting retirement goals is not a one-time task; it's an ongoing process. Regularly monitor your progress and reassess your goals as your circumstances change. Life events, financial conditions, and shifting priorities may require adjustments to your retirement objectives. Stay informed, adaptable, and committed to securing your financial future during retirement.

The Art of Budgeting

Think of the last time you cooked an unfamiliar dish without a recipe. Did it go well? Did the meal turn out fine? If yes, then that's great. You're skilled at improvisation. If it didn't, don't fret. It's normal to fail at something when you're just *winging* it. That's why, when it comes to personal finance, it's important to learn the art of budgeting. Essentially, sticking to a budget means following a recipe when it comes to managing your finances. If you don't stick to a budget, you're essentially just winging it could potentially end in disaster.

A budget is a financial plan that outlines your expected income and expenses over a specific period, typically on a monthly or yearly basis. It's a roadmap that helps you manage your money, control your spending, and achieve your financial goals. In retirement, having a well-structured budget is just as crucial as it is during your working years. A budget provides a clear view of your financial situation, ensuring you have control and awareness of your money. It also allows you to control your expenses, prevent overspending, and focus on what truly matters to you.

Now, let's dive into the key components of budgeting. We've already talked extensively about income. Now, let's use this section to explore the difference between Fixed and Variable Expenses.

Fixed Expenses are recurring costs that remain relatively constant month to month. Examples include mortgage or rent payments, insurance premiums, utility bills, and loan payments (like car loans or credit card minimum payments). Fixed expenses are essential and need to be covered regularly.

Variable Expenses are costs that fluctuate based on your choices and circumstances. These can include groceries, dining out, entertainment, travel, and discretionary spending. Variable expenses are typically more flexible and can be adjusted to fit your budget.

Balancing your fixed and variable expenses is key to creating a sustainable retirement budget. Fixed expenses are nonnegotiable, while variable expenses offer room for adjustments, especially when faced with income changes or financial goals. Again, there are many approaches to personal finance that apply to budgeting styles. Let's go over some of the most popular budgeting methods:

Traditional Budgeting

Traditional budgeting is the most conventional and straightforward method. It involves creating a detailed plan that tracks your income and all expenses, categorizing them into various spending categories. The key characteristics of traditional budgeting include:

- **Income Assessment**: You start by calculating your total monthly income from all sources.

- **Expense Categorization**: You create categories for your expenses, such as housing, utilities, transportation, groceries, and discretionary spending.

- **Expense Tracking**: You meticulously document all your expenses within each category over a specified period.

- **Budget Creation**: Using data from your expense tracking, you create a budget by assigning specific dollar amounts to each expense category, aiming to ensure your total expenses are less than your total income.

- **Review and Adjust**: You regularly review your budget to monitor your progress. If necessary, you make adjustments to stay on track.

Traditional budgeting provides a comprehensive view of your financial situation and is ideal for people who prefer detailed financial planning and a structured approach to managing their money.

Reverse Budgeting

Reverse budgeting focuses on saving and meeting financial goals before allocating money to expenses. This approach is characterized by the following:

- **Set Financial Goals**: You begin by defining your financial objectives, which could include saving for retirement, building an emergency fund, debt reduction, or other goals.

- **Automate Savings**: Money is automatically deducted from your income and directed toward savings and investment accounts to fulfill your financial goals.

- **Budget Expenses:**After savings contributions, you allocate the remaining income to cover your expenses, ensuring your financial goals are met before discretionary spending.

Reverse budgeting prioritizes saving and achieving financial goals, making it particularly useful for those who want to ensure consistent savings.

Zero-Based Budgeting

Zero-based budgeting assigns a specific purpose to every dollar of your income, ensuring that your budget balances zero. The distinct features of zero-based budgeting are as follows:

- **Categorize Expenses**: You categorize all your expenses, including fixed and variable costs.

- **Budget to Zero:**You allocate your income to each expense category, ensuring every dollar has a designated purpose.

- **Adjust as Needed**: Your budget is continually evaluated to maintain a zero balance. Adjustments are made if your expenses or income change.

Zero-based budgeting encourages a close examination of your spending habits, promotes financial discipline, and helps you understand where your money goes.

50-30-20 Budgeting

The 50-30-20 budgeting method, also known as the "balanced money formula," is a simplified budgeting approach that divides your after-tax income into three main categories, each allocated a specific percentage of your income:

50% for Needs: This category, representing 50% of your income, covers essential expenses or needs. These expenses typically include housing, utilities, groceries, transportation, insurance, and minimum debt payments. The 50% allocation ensures that you have a secure financial foundation with the ability to meet your basic living requirements.

30% for Wants: The "wants" category, occupying 30% of your income, encompasses discretionary spending and lifestyle choices. This includes expenses like dining out, entertainment, hobbies, travel, and other nonessential items. The 30% allocation provides flexibility and allows you to enjoy life without feeling overly constrained by your budget.

20% for Savings and Debt Repayment: The remaining 20% of your income is dedicated to savings, investments, and debt repayment. This portion is essential for building financial security and preparing for retirement. It includes contributions to retirement accounts, emergency savings, and paying down debts beyond the minimum required payments.

Each budgeting approach offers a different perspective on managing your finances and achieving your retirement goals. The choice between them depends on your personal preferences, financial situation, and long-term objectives. You may even find that these methods work best for your specific needs.

Tracking Your Spending

When we touched on expenses earlier, we talked about how they could be classified as fixed or variable. And that still holds true. But there's also a more nuanced approach to categorizing expenses by nature and not merely by frequency. It's important that you learn how to track your spending because this will give you an accurate insight into where your money goes. Aside from classifying expenses as either fixed or variable, you can also categorize them as either needs, wants, or savings/debt payments. See the end of the chapter for an expense tracker sheet.

Needs

Needs are essential expenses that are necessary for your basic survival and well-being. These expenses typically fall into the following categories:

- **Housing**: This includes your rent or mortgage payments, property taxes, home insurance, utilities (electricity, water, gas), and maintenance costs. Housing is a fundamental need, and it usually represents a significant portion of your budget.

- **Groceries**: Food and basic household items are essential for maintaining your health and daily life. Groceries encompass items like fresh produce, canned goods, meat, dairy, and toiletries.

- **Transportation**: Transportation costs are essential for getting to work, school, medical appointments, and running errands. They include expenses related to your car loan or lease, gas, public transportation, insurance, maintenance, and registration.

- **Healthcare**: This category covers health insurance premiums, doctor's visits, prescription medications, and other medical expenses. Access to healthcare is crucial for maintaining your physical well-being.

- **Minimum Debt Payments**: If you have outstanding debts, minimum debt payments are essential to avoid defaulting on loans or credit cards. They ensure you meet your financial obligations and avoid potential negative consequences.

- **Insurance**: Necessary insurance policies, such as health, auto, and homeowner's or renter's insurance, fall into the needs category as they provide protection and financial security.

- **Utilities**: These include electricity, water, gas, and other essential services required for day-to-day living. Utility bills are considered needs because they support your basic comfort and functionality.

Wants

Wants represent discretionary expenses that enhance your quality of life but are necessary for survival. These expenses can be luxurious in nature and often include:

- **Entertainment**: Spending on movies, dining out, concerts, recreational activities, and hobbies fall into the "wants" category. These expenses are not essential but contribute to your enjoyment and leisure.

- **Travel**: While some travel may be essential (e.g., commuting to work), vacations, weekend getaways, and other nonessential trips are considered wants. Travel expenses can be enjoyable but are not required for daily living.

- **Dining Out**: Eating at restaurants, ordering takeout, and enjoying gourmet meals are typical wants. While dining out can be a delightful experience, it's not essential for sustaining life.

- **Hobbies**: Pursuing personal interests and hobbies, whether it's collecting, crafting, or sports, is often categorized as a want. Hobbies contribute to your well-being and enjoyment.

- **Luxury Goods**: Purchases of luxury items like designer clothing, high-end electronics, or premium accessories are considered wants. These items are not essential for basic living.

- **Nonessential Subscriptions**: Subscriptions to streaming services, magazines, or other forms of entertainment are often categorized as wants. While they offer entertainment and convenience, they are not necessities.

Savings/Debt Repayments

This category is dedicated to securing your financial future and addressing outstanding financial obligations. It can look different from person to person depending on goals and current financial situations, but expenses that fall within this category may include:

- **Savings**: Contributions to savings accounts, retirement accounts, emergency funds, and other long-term financial goals fall into this category. Saving for the future is a crucial part of financial planning.

- **Debt Repayment**: Beyond minimum debt payments, additional contributions to paying down debts, such as credit cards, student loans, or personal loans, are allocated to this category. Reducing and eliminating debt is an essential financial goal.

Identifying Financial Leaks

A financial leak refers to unplanned, unnecessary, or avoidable expenses that, over time, can significantly drain your financial resources. These are often small, overlooked spending habits that, when aggregated, substantially impact your overall financial health. Financial leaks can be insidious because they may not be immediately obvious, yet they can undermine your financial stability and progress. It's important that you maintain hyper-awareness over how you're spending your money. Here are some of the most common financial leaks that you should be on the lookout for:

- **Impulse Purchases**: Impulse buying can lead to financial leaks as you spend on items you didn't plan to purchase. To plug this leak, practice mindful spending by creating shopping lists and waiting before making nonessential purchases.

- **Subscription Services**: Accumulating numerous subscription services for streaming, magazines, apps, and more can add up. Identify and cancel subscriptions you no longer use or need.

- **Dining Out**: Frequent dining out or takeout orders can be a substantial financial leak. Reduce dining expenses by cooking at home, meal planning, and limiting restaurant visits.

- **Unused Memberships**: Gym memberships, streaming platforms, or club memberships that you no longer use are financial leaks. Cancel underutilized memberships and reallocate the funds.

- **Late Fees and Interest**: Paying late fees and interest on credit cards or loans due to missed payments can drain your finances.

Set up reminders, automate payments, and improve your financial organization to prevent this leak.

- **Untracked Cash Expenses**: Cash spending that isn't accounted for can be a hidden leak. Track and budget for cash expenses to ensure they don't lead to financial leaks.

- **Overpriced Services**: Evaluate regular service providers like insurance, utilities, and cell phone plans. Compare options, negotiate for better rates, and switch providers if needed.

- **Online Shopping**: Online shopping can lead to impulsive purchases and financial leaks. Implement strategies like adding items to a wish list and practicing a waiting period before buying.

Understanding Retirement Accounts

Retirement accounts play a crucial role in securing your financial future during retirement. A 401(k) plan is a popular retirement savings vehicle offered by many employers. It falls under defined contribution plans, meaning that you and your employer can contribute to the account. Essentially, it works: you, as an employee, can elect to contribute a portion of your pre-tax salary to your 401(k) account, reducing your taxable income for the year. The funds you contribute are invested in options, such as mutual funds, stocks, and bonds, depending on the plan's offerings. Many employers also offer a matching contribution, where they will match a portion of your contributions up to a certain limit. This is essentially free money for your retirement savings.

One of the key advantages of a 401(k) is the tax benefits. Your contributions are tax-deductible, reducing your taxable income in the year you contribute. This allows your investments to grow tax-deferred until you make withdrawals in retirement. At that point, the withdrawals are taxed as ordinary income. While a 401(k) offers excellent tax benefits, it also comes with restrictions. Withdrawals before age 59½ may incur a penalty, except for specific situations, like disability or certain early withdrawals for home purchases or education expenses. After age 72, required minimum distributions (RMDs) must begin, and you must start withdrawing a minimum amount each year.

Another alternative to a retirement account you might be familiar with is the IRA. An IRA, or Individual Retirement Account, is another valuable retirement savings tool you can open independently. Unlike a 401(k), which is typically employer-sponsored, an IRA is opened and managed by an individual. You have more control over the investment choices and can choose from a broader range of investment options. IRAs have annual contribution limits set by the IRS, which are generally lower than those for 401(k)s. However, they offer more flexibility because you can choose where to open your IRA and have a wide range of investment choices.

IRAs provide tax benefits similar to a 401(k). Traditional IRAs offer tax-deductible contributions and tax-deferred growth, while Roth IRAs use after-tax contributions and offer tax-free withdrawals in retirement. Traditional IRAs typically have a penalty for early withdrawals before age 59½. However, Roth IRAs allow you to withdraw your contributions (but not earnings) at any time without penalties. IRAs are often used for rollovers from 401(k) plans when you change jobs or retire. This allows you to continue growing your retirement savings independently.

In addition to the 401(k) and IRAs, there are several other retirement account options that retirees can consider, each with its unique features and advantages. It's essential to be aware of these alternatives to make well-informed decisions about your retirement savings. Traditional pensions, often provided by employers, promise retirees a specific monthly benefit based on factors like years of service and salary history. These plans are a valuable source of retirement income and provide financial security in retirement. However, they are becoming less common in the private sector.

There are also 403(b) plans that are typically offered by nonprofit organizations and educational institutions, such as schools and hospitals. They function similarly to 401(k) plans, allowing employees to make tax-deferred contributions toward their retirement. Employers may also offer matching contributions or contributions on behalf of the employee. GIAs or Guaranteed Income Annuities, including the Thrift Savings Plan (TSP) for federal employees, are another form of defined contribution plan where contributions are invested and can grow tax deferred. They offer a range of investment options and allow you to tailor your investments based on your risk tolerance and goals.

Taxes After Retirement?

Retirement does not necessarily mean the end of your tax obligations, but the tax landscape changes, and understanding how it affects your retirement income is crucial. The type and amount of taxes you'll pay in retirement can vary based on factors such as your income sources, location, and the specific tax laws in your state. Here's a breakdown of some key tax considerations for retirees:

- **Federal Income Tax**: In retirement, your sources of income may include Social Security, pensions, retirement account withdrawals (like 401(k) or IRA), and investment income. Social Security benefits can be partially taxable based on your total income. Pension income and withdrawals from tax-deferred retirement accounts are generally taxable. Investment income may also be subject to capital gains tax. Your overall federal tax liability will depend on your total income, deductions, and credits.

- **State Income Tax:** The taxation of retirement income at the state level varies widely. Some states, like Florida, Texas, and Nevada, have no state income tax, making them popular choices for retirees. Others may tax specific types of retirement income, such as pensions or Social Security. Research the tax laws in your state of residence and consider the tax implications of moving to a tax-friendlier state in retirement.

- **Property Tax**: Property taxes can be a significant financial burden for homeowners. Some states offer property tax relief programs for seniors, which can reduce the property tax burden. Research whether your state offers such programs and explore the eligibility criteria.

- **Estate and Inheritance Taxes**: Not all states impose estate or inheritance taxes, but if they do, these taxes can impact your estate planning. Consulting with an estate planning attorney can help you understand the implications of these taxes and create a plan to minimize them.

- **Sales Tax**: Sales tax rates can also vary by state. Some states exempt certain items or provide reduced rates for seniors. Be aware of the sales tax laws in your state and consider your spending patterns.

- **Tax-Efficient Withdrawal Strategies**: Managing your retirement withdrawals wisely can reduce your tax liability. Consider strategies like tax-efficient distribution of retirement account withdrawals, including Roth conversions, and taking advantage of lower tax brackets in retirement.

- **Qualified Retirement Accounts (QCDs)**: If you're 70½ or older, you can make tax-free charitable donations directly from your IRA through Qualified Charitable Distributions (QCDs). This can reduce your taxable income while supporting causes you care about.

Tax laws are complex and ever-changing. It's advisable to consult a tax professional or financial advisor who specializes in retirement planning to ensure you make tax-efficient decisions in retirement.

Ultimately, understanding your tax situation in retirement and exploring strategies to minimize your tax liability can help you make the most of your retirement income. Additionally, considering relocation to a state with tax benefits can be a strategic financial move, but it's essential to evaluate all aspects, including the cost of living and quality of life, before making such a decision.

Maximizing Social Security

Social Security is a vital federal program designed to provide financial assistance and security to individuals and families, especially retirees, disabled individuals, and survivors of deceased workers. Ultimately, it's a government service that ensures that certain marginalized sectors of society never feel neglected or left behind.

To qualify for Social Security benefits, you typically need to accumulate a specific number of work credits. You earn work credits based on your work history and earnings. In 2023, you earn one credit for every $1,640 in earnings, up to a maximum of four credits per year. The number of credits required for different benefits varies. Here's a quick rundown:

- **Retirement Benefits**: Social Security retirement benefits are available to individuals who have reached full retirement age (FRA), which is currently 67 for those born in 1960 or later. You can choose to begin receiving benefits as early as age 62, but your monthly benefit amount will be reduced if you start before your FRA. Delaying benefits until after your FRA can increase your monthly benefit.

- **Disability Benefits**: Social Security provides financial support to individuals with disabilities who meet specific medical and work-related criteria. You must have a severe disability expected to last at least 12 months or result in death. Additionally, you need to have earned a certain number of work credits, depending on your age at the onset of the disability.

- **Survivor Benefits**: Survivors of deceased workers, including widows, widowers, and dependent children, may be eligible for survivors' benefits. Eligibility criteria vary, but typically, survivors receive a percentage of the deceased worker's benefit amount.

Calculating your Social Security benefits can be a bit complex. Your Social Security benefit is based on your highest-earning 35 years of work. The Social Security Administration (SSA) indexes your past earnings to account for inflation and calculates your average indexed monthly earnings (AIME). The AIME is then used to determine your primary insurance amount (PIA), which represents the full retirement benefit you'd receive at your full retirement age. If you choose to receive benefits before or after your FRA, your monthly benefit amount will be adjusted accordingly.

You can begin receiving Social Security retirement benefits as early as age 62 or as late as age 70. The age at which you claim benefits affects the monthly benefit amount. Claiming early results in reduced monthly benefits, while delaying can increase your benefits. The decision of when to claim depends on your individual circumstances, including your health, financial needs, and retirement plans.

Chapter Conclusion

Money is a serious issue, especially as you grow older. While there's a certain taboo attached to discussions about finance, it's important that we are able to break out of our shells and talk about money in a way that's healthy and productive. In this chapter, we made an effort to better understand our current financial situation, delving into personal financial statements, assets, liabilities, income, and expenses. We also discussed the importance of setting retirement goals, budgeting, and identifying financial leaks to ensure a secure financial future.

Furthermore, we explored various retirement accounts, including 401(k)s and IRAs, to help you make informed decisions about your savings. We also looked at other retirement options and the potential tax implications of your choices. Social Security became a pivotal part of our discussion as we examined how benefits are calculated and the best practices for claiming strategies.

Ultimately, it's important to remember that your financial well-being is a fundamental aspect of a blissful retirement. Understanding your financial situation, setting clear goals, and making informed decisions about your income sources are key steps toward achieving your retirement dreams.

In the next chapter, we'll shift our focus to community involvement and giving back to society. We'll explore how staying active and engaged in your community can enrich your retirement experience and add meaning to your life.

Expense Tracker

Month:
Year:

Date	Description	Amount	Balance
		Total:	

Notes:

THE GIFT OF GIVING BACK - VOLUNTEERING AND PHILANTHROPY

L ife's most persistent and urgent question is: What are you doing for others? –Martin Luther King Jr.

Retirement offers a unique opportunity, a phase in life where you can redirect your energy, experience, and skills toward making a positive impact on the world. It's a time to reflect on the profound question: "What are you doing for others?" As you enter this chapter, we'll explore the joy and fulfillment that comes from community involvement, volunteering, and philanthropy.

By giving back to your community and contributing to causes you're passionate about, you not only enrich the lives of those you touch but also experience a profound sense of purpose and connection that adds immense value to your retirement. Your retirement years can be more than just relaxation and leisure; they can be a time of meaningful action and positive change.

Community Involvement After Retirement

Just because you're getting older doesn't mean that you have less to contribute to the world. In fact, the opposite is often true! There's a wide array of opportunities waiting for you, each offering a unique and meaningful way to give back to society. Here's a glimpse of what you might encounter:

- **Community Organizations**:Many local organizations, such as charities, nonprofits, and community centers, welcome volunteers with open arms. These organizations often host events, provide support to the less fortunate, and engage in various community development activities. Your time and expertise can be invaluable to them.

- **Mentorship Programs**:Schools and educational institutions frequently seek experienced individuals to mentor students, helping them navigate their educational journeys. Sharing your knowledge and wisdom can be incredibly fulfilling.

- **Environmental Initiatives**: If you're passionate about the environment, you can participate in local clean-up drives and conservation efforts or join gardening clubs to beautify your community.

- **Health and Wellness**: Retirement is an excellent time to support your local health organizations or participate in fitness and wellness programs. You can offer guidance to individuals looking to lead healthier lives, which, in turn, enhances your well-being.

- **Arts and Culture**:Many artistic and cultural institutions, such as museums, theaters, and libraries, thrive on the support of volunteers. You can share your love for the arts by contributing your time or skills.

- **Faith-Based Activities**: If you're a member of a religious community, there are numerous opportunities for involvement, from participating in outreach programs to volunteering within your congregation.

- **Social Clubs and Senior Centers**: Many retirees enjoy the camaraderie and activities offered by senior centers and social clubs. These centers often host events, classes, and activities that help you stay engaged and active in your community.

The possibilities are endless, and you can choose activities that align with your interests, passions, and the causes you hold dear. Community involvement and volunteering in retirement offer a plethora of benefits that can significantly enhance your overall well-being. Here are some of the key advantages to consider:

- **Sense of Purpose**: Volunteering provides you with a sense of purpose and fulfillment, which can combat feelings of isolation and depression that some retirees may experience.

- **Mental Stimulation**: Engaging in new activities and challenges stimulates your brain and keeps it active, reducing the risk of cognitive decline.

- **Social Connections**: Volunteering often involves working with others, forging new friendships, and maintaining a robust social network. Social interactions can boost your mood and provide a sense of belonging.

- **Physical Activity**: Many volunteer opportunities are physically engaging, which can help you stay active and maintain your physical health. This can reduce the risk of age-related health issues.

- **Stress Reduction**: Volunteering can help reduce stress, improve your overall mood, and increase your emotional well-being. Lower stress levels can positively impact your heart health and overall longevity.

- **Tax Benefits:** Depending on your location and the nature of your volunteer work, you may be eligible for certain tax deductions or credits. These can provide financial relief in retirement.

- **Savings on Entertainment**: Volunteering often comes with access to various events or activities at a reduced cost or even for free. This can help you enjoy leisure activities without breaking the bank.

- **New Skills and Opportunities**: Volunteering can also be an opportunity to acquire new skills or explore potential career paths in retirement. This might lead to part-time or consulting work, supplementing your retirement income.

In addition to these benefits, volunteering allows you to give back to your community and make a positive impact on the lives of others. It's a win-win situation, where you benefit both personally and through the positive changes you bring to your community. Whether you want to support educational initiatives, help those in need, or share your skills, there's a volunteer opportunity out there that's a perfect match for you.

How to Make an Impact in Retirement

Making an impact in retirement doesn't have to mean donating millions of dollars to charities. You can make an impact even by just spending an hour every week or so contributing toward community efforts. It can be an incredibly rewarding and meaningful experience when you participate in volunteerism and community service campaigns. And in order to make the most out of your volunteer efforts, here are a few things that you should stay mindful of:

- Choose volunteer opportunities that align with your interests, skills, and passions. When you're passionate about the cause, you're more likely to stay committed and make a significant impact.

- Explore various organizations and their volunteer programs to find the right fit. Learn about their missions, objectives, and the specific roles they offer. Consider the size and reputation of the organization.

- Assess how much time you can realistically dedicate to volunteering. Be clear about your availability and choose opportunities that match your schedule.

- Define what you want to achieve through your volunteer work. Whether it's helping a certain number of people, contributing to a specific project, or learning new skills, having goals can keep you motivated.

- Maintain open and honest communication with the organization and the people you're helping. Ask questions, share your ideas, and express any concerns or suggestions.

- Consistency is key. Show up on time and fulfill your commitments. Reliable volunteers are highly valued by organizations.

- Be open to working with diverse groups of people, including those with different backgrounds, beliefs, and experiences. Embrace the opportunity to learn from others.

- Many volunteer roles involve access to sensitive information. Respect the privacy and confidentiality of the people you're assisting and the organization you're working with.

- Set a positive example for fellow volunteers by demonstrating kindness, empathy, and a strong work ethic. Your attitude and behavior can inspire others.

- Periodically assess your volunteer experience. Reflect on what you've achieved and whether your goals are being met. Use this self-reflection to make improvements and maximize your impact.

- Form connections with both the people you're helping and your fellow volunteers. Building relationships can enhance the sense of community and increase the effectiveness of your efforts.

- Remember that the impact you make might not always be immediately visible, but your contributions can lead to positive changes in your community over time. Stay committed, and stay passionate, and your volunteer work will continue to benefit those you serve and yourself.

Meaningful Ways to Volunteer

"As you grow older, you will discover you have two hands — one for helping yourself, the other for helping others." –Audrey Hepburn

Again, there are so many opportunities that are out there when it comes to volunteerism and advocacy. But if you don't necessarily know what you would like to get yourself into just yet, that's fine. Here are a few ideas that you can consider:

- **Habitat for Humanity**: Habitat for Humanity is known for its mission of providing affordable housing to those in need. Retirees can contribute by volunteering to build or repair homes for families, which can be an immensely rewarding experience.

- **Helping Troops and Veterans**: Retirees can support military troops and veterans in various ways, such as sending care packages, offering job placement assistance, or volunteering at veterans' organizations to provide companionship and support.

- **Working With Children**: Volunteering with children can involve reading at local schools, mentoring young people, or assisting in after-school programs. Retirees' life experiences and wisdom make them excellent role models.

- **Volunteer Vacations**: Combine travel with volunteering by participating in volunteer vacations. Retirees can embark on journeys to other countries or within their own nation, engaging in community projects while exploring new places.

- **Hunger Relief**: Joining a local food bank, shelter, or hunger relief organization can be a meaningful way to address food insecurity in the community. Activities might include food distribution, meal preparation, or fundraising.

- **Disaster Relief**: Retirees can become disaster response volunteers, helping communities recover from natural disasters. Training in disaster relief preparedness may be necessary, but the ability to provide aid when needed is invaluable.

- **Political Campaigns**: Get involved in local or national politics by volunteering for political campaigns. This might entail activities such as canvassing, phone banking, or organizing events to promote a cause or candidate you believe in.

- **Animal Shelters**: If you're an animal lover, consider volunteering at an animal shelter. Duties could range from walking dogs and feeding cats to helping with adoption events and providing care and companionship to animals in need.

Each of these causes and advocacies offers unique opportunities to make a difference, and you can choose one that most resonates with your interests and personal advocacies. Community service can be an incredibly fulfilling way to spend your time in retirement. You would be surprised at how much dedicating your time and energy to the service of others can be so rewarding for your soul.

Chapter Conclusion

Hopefully, this chapter will have opened your eyes to the wonderful world of charitable efforts and volunteering for the sake of community development. Community involvement after retirement is more than just an option; it's an opportunity to give back, connect with others, and find deeper meaning in your retired life. Whether you choose to volunteer for a cause that resonates with your values or engage in a broader range of activities, the benefits are boundless.

Not only does community involvement contribute to the betterment of society, but it also enhances your own well-being. Engaging with others, sharing your skills and experiences, and working toward a common goal can boost your mental and physical health, provide a sense of fulfillment, and foster new friendships in your retirement years.

In our next chapter, we'll shift our focus to another vital aspect of retirement – your physical health and well-being. We'll discuss healthcare costs in retirement, the benefits of Health Savings Accounts (HSAs), and ways to maintain a healthy and active lifestyle. Your retirement is a time for thriving, and we'll provide you with the knowledge and insights to do just that. So, let's explore the path to a healthier and more fulfilling retirement together.

STAYING HEALTHY AND HAPPY

In the quest for a fulfilling retirement, we often concentrate on the financial aspects - ensuring our savings are in order, investment portfolios are stable, and budgets are well-planned. Yet, amidst these financial preparations, a fundamental aspect can't be overlooked: your physical health and well-being. In this chapter, we will explore the critical components of staying healthy and happy in retirement. While the financial side is essential, your health plays an equally significant role in shaping your retirement experience. After all, what good is a well-padded bank account if you're not in good health to enjoy it?

Just as you've prepared wisely for your financial future, it's equally crucial to take charge of your physical and emotional well-being. Your health is an invaluable asset, and this chapter is your guide to nurturing it during your retirement journey. So, let's embark on this path to a healthier and happier retirement together.

Physical Health and Well-Being

Healthcare Costs

You might be wondering just how much money you need to prepare in order for you to stay healthy in retirement. And while that's certainly a good way to prepare yourself financially, the answer isn't always so cut and dry. There are so many factors that you need to take into consideration when calculating your expected healthcare costs in retirement, such as:

- **Healthcare Inflation**: One of the primary factors influencing healthcare costs is inflation within the healthcare sector. Healthcare costs tend to rise at a rate higher than the general inflation rate, making it essential to prepare for increased expenses over time.

- **Age-Related Expenses**: As we age, our healthcare needs often increase. Older adults may require more frequent medical visits, diagnostic tests, and treatments, which can contribute to higher healthcare costs.

- **Choice of Healthcare Plan**: The type of healthcare plan you choose during retirement can significantly impact your costs. Medicare, for instance, offers various plans, each with different coverage and cost structures. Understanding the nuances of these plans is vital for managing expenses.

- **Long-Term Care**: Long-term care, such as nursing home or assisted living facility stays, can be a substantial financial burden.

It's essential to assess your potential long-term care needs and plan accordingly.

- **Prescription Medications**: The cost of prescription medications can vary widely, and some retirees may require expensive medications to manage chronic conditions. Exploring options for prescription drug coverage is critical in managing this aspect of healthcare expenses.

- **Dental and Vision Care**: Many traditional healthcare plans don't provide comprehensive dental and vision coverage. Retirees may need separate coverage for these areas, which adds to their healthcare expenses.

- **Geographic Location**: Your place of residence during retirement can also influence healthcare costs. Different regions may have varying healthcare price structures, so consider these regional disparities when planning.

- **Overall Health and Lifestyle**: Maintaining a healthy lifestyle can significantly impact healthcare costs. Regular exercise, a balanced diet, and stress management can help reduce the need for medical care and medications.

- Again, healthcare costs can look very different for every retiree, but let's try to look at this hypothetical case for a subject that we will call Susan. She is 65, lives in an urban area with relatively moderate healthcare costs, and is generally healthy, save for some minor age-related health issues. She is fully enrolled in Medicare and has supplemental Medigap coverage.

- **Medicare Premiums Medicare Part A (Hospital Insurance)**: is premium-free for most retirees who complete around 10 years of payments through employment, but Part B (Medical Insurance) comes with a monthly premium. In 2023, the standard Part B premium is $170.10 per month. Susan pays this premium each month for comprehensive medical coverage.

- **Supplemental Insurance (Medigap)**: Susan has chosen to enroll in a Medigap plan, which helps cover the out-of-pocket costs associated with Medicare. The cost of Medigap policies varies but can range from around $100 to $300 per month. Susan pays an additional $150 per month for her Medigap coverage.

- **Prescription Drug Coverage (Part D)**: Medicare Part D offers prescription drug coverage. The cost of Part D plans varies based on the specific plan and the medications covered. Susan's Part D plan costs her an additional $40 per month.

- **Copayments and Deductibles:** Susan visits her primary care physician and specialists regularly for check-ups and management of her health conditions. She incurs copayments of around $20 for each visit. In addition, her plan requires her to meet a deductible of $250 per year.

- **Dental and Vision Care**: Susan has a separate dental and vision insurance plan, which costs her an extra $50 per month.

- **Additional Health-Related Expenses**: Susan also budgets for wellness programs, fitness classes, and over-the-counter medications, which add an additional $100 per month.

- **Long-Term Care Insurance**: Susan has long-term care insurance, which costs her $200 per month. This policy covers potential long-term care needs, including nursing home or assisted living care.

Again, this is a very specific estimate for a hypothetical case. Your needs may vary and can be significantly less or more than what Susan spends on her healthcare. Ultimately, it's important that you know what to expect to pay in retirement for your healthcare in order for you to be able to prepare for it financially. Retirement isn't just about going on vacation and pursuing your dreams. It's also about ensuring that you stay healthy enough to do everything that you want to do for a long time. Here are a few tips on how you can effectively plan and prepare for your retirement health insurance costs:

Effectively planning and preparing for retirement health insurance costs is essential for maintaining financial stability and well-being during your retirement years. Here are some tips to help you navigate the complexities of health insurance in retirement:

- **Understand Medicare**: Medicare is the federal health insurance program for individuals aged 65 and older. It consists of different parts, including Part A (hospital insurance), Part B (medical insurance), Part C (Medicare Advantage), and Part D (prescription drug coverage). Understanding the basics of Medicare is crucial as it serves as the foundation of health coverage for most retirees.

- **Enroll in Medicare on Time**: You become eligible for Medicare at age 65. To avoid potential penalties, make sure to enroll in Medicare Part B within the Initial Enrollment Period, which begins three months before your 65th birthday and extends for seven months. Missing this window could lead to higher premiums.

- **Consider Supplemental Coverage**: Original Medicare (Parts A and B) doesn't cover all healthcare costs. To fill the gaps, you may consider supplemental insurance, such as Medigap (Medicare Supplemental Insurance) or Medicare Advantage plans. These plans can help reduce out-of-pocket expenses.

- **Evaluate Prescription Drug Coverage**: Medicare Part D provides prescription drug coverage. You can choose a Part D plan that aligns with your medication needs. Compare available plans to find one that offers coverage for your specific medications at a reasonable cost.

- **Plan for Long-Term Care**: Medicare does not typically cover long-term care, such as nursing home or assisted living facility expenses. Consider long-term care insurance to help protect your assets and ensure you receive the care you need without depleting your savings.

- **Compare Advantage Plans**: Medicare Advantage plans are offered by private insurers and provide an alternative to Original Medicare. These plans may offer additional benefits like dental, vision, and hearing coverage. Carefully assess whether they align with your healthcare needs and budget.

- **Monitor Health Expenses**: Track your health expenses regularly to understand your healthcare spending patterns. This can help you identify areas where you can potentially reduce costs.

- **Budget for Healthcare**: Include healthcare expenses in your overall retirement budget. Account for Medicare premiums, supplemental insurance, prescription drug costs, and any health-related expenses like copays and deductibles.

- **Save for Healthcare Costs**: Open a Health Savings Account (HSA)with a High Deductible Health Plan (HDHP). HSAs offer tax benefits and can be used to pay for eligible healthcare expenses in retirement. We'll talk more about HSAs later on.

- **Explore Medicaid**: If your income and assets are limited, you may qualify for Medicaid, which can provide healthcare coverage at a low or no cost.

- **Stay Healthy**: Prioritize preventive care, a healthy lifestyle, and exercise to minimize health issues that can lead to higher healthcare expenses.

- **Regularly Review Your Coverage**:Health insurance options, healthcare needs, and financial situation can change over time. Periodically review your coverage and adjust it as necessary.

Again, a person's needs can vary depending on each specific case. You don't have to concern yourself with all of these details if you don't have to. But knowledge is power, and it's always best that you stay aware of all your options so that you are able to make informed decisions whenever necessary.

HSA for Retirement

A Health Savings Account (HSA) is a tax-advantaged financial account designed to help individuals save for qualified medical expenses, both now and in retirement. HSAs are available to individuals who are enrolled in a High Deductible Health Plan (HDHP), a specific type of health insurance plan characterized by its higher deductible and lower premiums.

Now, how do you stand to benefit from making use of HSAs for retirement?

- **Tax Advantages**: One of the primary benefits of an HSA is its tax advantages. Contributions to an HSA are tax-deductible, reducing your taxable income for the year in which you make contributions. Additionally, the interest or investment earnings on the funds within the HSA grow tax-free, and withdrawals used for qualified medical expenses are tax-free as well. This triple tax advantage makes HSAs a powerful tool for healthcare savings.

- **Ownership and Portability**:HSAs are owned by the individual, not the employer. This means that you can take your HSA with you when you change jobs or retire. The account is not tied to a specific employer or insurance plan.

- **Triple Use**: HSAs offer flexibility in how you can use the funds. You can use them for qualified medical expenses, which can include doctor's visits, hospital bills, prescription medications, and other healthcare costs. Additionally, you can use HSA funds for dental and vision expenses. Importantly, once you reach age 65, you can also withdraw funds from your HSA for nonmedical expenses without penalty, although regular income tax applies.

- **No Use-It-Or-Lose-It Rule**: Unlike some other types of accounts, HSAs do not have a use-it-or-lose-it rule. The funds you contribute to an HSA remain in the account and continue to grow year after year. This makes it a suitable vehicle for saving for healthcare expenses in retirement.

- **Portability**: HSAs are portable, which means you can keep your account and your funds even if you change jobs or health insurance plans. This ensures your savings continue to grow regardless of your employment status.

- **Contribution Limits**: The IRS sets annual contribution limits for HSAs. These limits are typically adjusted for inflation. You can contribute the maximum allowed amount each year to maximize the tax benefits.

- **Catch-up Contributions**: Individuals aged 55 and older can make additional catch-up contributions to their HSA, allowing them to save more for healthcare expenses in retirement.

- **Investment Options**:Some HSA providers offer investment options that allow you to invest your HSA funds in various assets like stocks, bonds, and mutual funds, potentially leading to higher returns over time.

- **Beneficiary Designation**: You can designate a beneficiary who will inherit your HSA upon your passing, and the account retains its tax advantages even after your death.

- **Use for Medicare Premiums:** After you turn 65, you can use HSA funds for Medicare premiums (not including premiums for Medicare Supplement or Medigap insurance) and long-term care insurance premiums.

HSAs are a valuable tool for saving healthcare expenses during retirement, as they offer tax advantages, flexibility, and investment opportunities. However, not everyone is eligible to open an HSA. Eligibility is based on several key criteria, including specific requirements related to your health insurance plan and your personal tax status. To be eligible for an HSA, you must meet the following requirements:

- **Enrollment in a High Deductible Health Plan (HDHP)**: To qualify for an HSA, you must be covered by a High Deductible Health Plan (HDHP). An HDHP is a specific type of health insurance plan characterized by its higher deductible and typically lower premiums compared to traditional health insurance plans.

- **HDHP Minimum Deductible**: The HDHP you're enrolled in must meet the minimum deductible requirement set by the Internal Revenue Service (IRS). The minimum deductible can change annually and may vary for self-only and family coverage.

- **No Other Health Coverage**: To be HSA-eligible, you generally cannot have other health coverage that is not an HDHP. Some exceptions exist, such as coverage for specific illnesses or accidents, as well as dental, vision, long-term care, and certain types of insurance, like disability or worker's compensation.

- **Not Enrolled in Medicare**: You are not eligible for an HSA if you are enrolled in Medicare. This means that HSA eligibility usually ends when you turn 65 and enroll in Medicare. It's important to note that contributions to an HSA can continue, but the funds can no longer be used tax-free for Medicare premiums, although they can still be used for qualified medical expenses.

- **Not Claimed as a Dependent**: If someone else can claim you as a dependent on their tax return, you are not eligible for an HSA. Being claimed as a dependent affects your personal tax status and changes your eligibility for contributing to an HSA.

- **HSA Contribution Limits**: You must adhere to annual HSA contribution limits set by the IRS. These limits can change from year to year and are usually adjusted for inflation. It's essential to monitor your contributions to ensure you don't exceed these limits.

- **HSA Catch-Up Contributions (if applicable)**: Individuals aged 55 and older are eligible to make additional catch-up contributions to their HSA. This is an extra contribution allowed by the IRS, providing older individuals with the opportunity to save more for healthcare expenses in retirement.

It's important to verify your HSA eligibility status based on the specific details of your health insurance plan and your personal circumstances. If you meet these eligibility criteria, you can open and contribute to an HSA. It's crucial to maximize the tax advantages that come with HSA contributions and use the funds for qualified medical expenses, both in the present and during your retirement years.

How to Stay Healthy in Retirement

When it comes to staying healthy, it's never easy. It requires a lot of discipline and commitment. But it doesn't have to be a hassle. It's just a matter of incorporating good habits into your everyday routine. You don't have to deprive yourself of the joys of life. You just have to try to take everything in moderation. Don't overindulge, but don't deprive yourself of fully experiencing life.

- **Staying Active**: Regular physical activity is vital for maintaining health in retirement. Incorporate a mix of aerobic exercises, strength training, flexibility exercises, and balance exercises into your routine. Activities like walking, swimming, yoga, and dancing can be enjoyable and beneficial.

- **Get Enough Sleep**: Quality sleep is essential for overall well-being. Aim for 7-9 hours of restful sleep each night. Create a comfortable sleep environment, establish a regular sleep schedule, and practice relaxation techniques to improve sleep quality.

- **Eat Healthy**: Your diet plays a crucial role in your health. Focus on a balanced diet that includes plenty of fruits, vegetables, whole grains, lean proteins, and healthy fats. Minimize processed foods, excessive sugar, and salt intake. Stay hydrated and consider any dietary restrictions or specific nutritional needs based on your health.

- **Reduce Alcohol Intake**: Limit alcohol consumption. While some studies suggest that moderate alcohol consumption may have certain health benefits, excessive drinking can lead to various health issues. If you choose to drink, do so in moderation and consult with your healthcare provider about what's safe for you.

- **Play Games**: Engage in mental activities like puzzles, board games, or brain-teaser games. They can help keep your mind sharp and provide enjoyable social interactions.

- **Pick Up New Skills**: Learning something new, whether it's a musical instrument, a new language, or a craft, can be both mentally stimulating and satisfying. Lifelong learning is a fantastic way to stay engaged and fulfilled.

- **Build and Maintain Social Connections**: Strong social connections are associated with improved mental and emotional health. Seek opportunities for social interaction, whether it's through joining clubs, volunteering, or simply staying in touch with friends and family.

- **Have a Wellness Plan**: Create a wellness plan tailored to your needs and preferences. Consider preventive healthcare measures, such as regular check-ups and screenings, and discuss your health goals with a healthcare provider. Your wellness plan should encompass physical, mental, and emotional well-being.

Again, prevention is always best when it comes to health care. You don't want just to prepare yourself in case you ever get sick. You want to avoid sickness at all costs. And while no one is immortal, you can do your best to maintain a healthy and active lifestyle in order to make yourself more formidable against the degenerative nature of aging.

Nutrition and Overall Well-Being

Remember, everyone's nutritional needs and wellness goals are unique. It's essential to tailor your approach to what works best for your health and lifestyle. Always consult a healthcare provider for personalized guidance on nutrition and wellness to ensure your retirement years are happy, healthy, and fulfilling. However, for the most part, these are the ideal principles that you should look to integrate into your daily life:

Good Dietary Habits:

- Focus on a diet rich in fruits, vegetables, whole grains, lean proteins, and healthy fats. This provides essential nutrients and helps maintain a healthy weight.

- Minimize processed foods, sugary snacks, and high-sodium items in your diet. These can contribute to chronic health issues.

- Stay hydrated by drinking an adequate amount of water each day.

- Be mindful of portion sizes to avoid overeating. Smaller, balanced meals can help prevent weight gain.

- Use smaller plates and utensils to create the illusion of larger portions.

- Establish a routine for regular meals. Skipping meals can lead to overeating later in the day.

- Include a variety of foods in your diet to ensure you get a wide range of nutrients.

- Choose healthy snacks like fruits, nuts, and yogurt to curb hunger between meals.

- Avoid empty-calorie snacks high in sugars and unhealthy fats.

Promote Emotional Well-Being:

- Incorporate regular physical activity into your routine. Aim for a mix of aerobic exercises, strength training, flexibility exercises, and balance exercises.

- Choose activities you enjoy to maintain motivation.

- Practice stress management techniques like meditation, yoga, or deep breathing exercises.

- Stay connected with friends and family to support your emotional and mental health.

- Keep up with the latest information regarding health and wellness.

- Pursue hobbies and interests that bring you joy and fulfillment.

- Enjoy the small moments in life and maintain a positive outlook.

- Ultimately, there are many approaches to staying healthy and happy in life. You just have to look for the one that works best for you because that would be the best way to sustain all these good habits.

Chapter Conclusion

While talking about health insurance and hospital bills can be scary, it's a necessary topic that we need to discuss as we prepare for old age. No one can beat Father Time. Eventually, our bodies will move farther and farther away from being in their prime. It's important that we are able to prepare ourselves for when we grow older and slower, and that doesn't necessarily have to be a bad or sad thing.

As we move forward, we will explore another significant dimension of retirement planning: estate planning and wealth transfer strategies. This chapter will guide you in creating a meaningful legacy and ensuring your assets are managed as per your wishes, securing your financial well-being for generations to come. So, stay with us as we continue our journey towards a fulfilling and prosperous retirement.

Your Legacy - Leaving a Lasting Mark

I n the twilight of your journey, it's time to reflect on the legacy you want to leave behind. Legacy isn't just about the assets you pass on; it's about the principles, values, and impact you leave on the world. This final chapter is dedicated to helping you create a lasting mark, ensuring your wishes are carried forward and that your loved ones are protected and provided for.

As we explore estate planning and wealth transfer strategies, let us contemplate the enduring values and principles we want to impart and the footprints we aim to leave behind. Your legacy is your story, the values you cherish, the wisdom you've gathered, and the love you've shared.

The Idea of Creating a Meaningful Legacy in Retirement

Legacy, in its most profound sense, is a testament to a life well-lived, a reflection of the values and principles that guided you and the impact you've had on the world. In the context of retirement, creating a meaningful legacy is not just about material wealth; it's about passing on your wisdom, values, and cherished principles to future generations.

Defining your legacy is a personal journey. It's about contemplating the principles you hold dear, the wisdom you've accumulated over the years, and the impact you want to leave behind. Your legacy might be about family values, social contributions, philanthropy, or simply the shared memories and stories that will endure for generations.

Take the time to reflect on your legacy and what you want it to encompass. Do you envision leaving behind a wealth of knowledge through journals and writings? Is your legacy focused on supporting causes that are close to your heart? Or is it about ensuring a secure financial future for your loved ones? Defining what legacy means to you lays the foundation for creating a lasting impact and ensuring your retirement years are filled with purpose and meaning.

The Work of Legacy Planning

Legacy planning is a process that goes beyond merely distributing assets and wealth; it encompasses the values, wisdom, and stories you want to pass down. To understand the work of legacy planning, it's essential to explore its history.

Share the History

Legacy planning has evolved over time. It used to primarily focus on passing down assets and wealth from one generation to the next. But in the modern sense, it encompasses transferring values and wisdom and preserving family stories. It's a holistic approach that considers legacy's emotional and intellectual elements.

Involve the Whole Family

Legacy planning isn't a solo endeavor. It involves your entire family. Encourage open discussions about your values, principles, and intentions for the future. Include your family members in these conversations so they understand your wishes and can contribute their own perspectives. Legacy planning should be a collective effort, reinforcing the sense of family unity.

Be Patient

Legacy planning is a journey, not a destination. It requires patience and ongoing effort. It might take time to crystallize your vision, communicate it to your loved ones, and ensure all the legal and financial aspects are in place. Be patient with yourself and your family throughout this process, as it's an investment in a meaningful and lasting legacy.

Ideas for Creating Your Legacy

Creating a meaningful legacy in retirement involves various avenues to express your values, wisdom, and experiences. Don't ever be deluded into thinking that this is some kind of narcissistic or vain affair. Your legacy is something that you've worked on and built all throughout your life. There's nothing wrong with wanting to leave it in the right hands and in the right way. Here are some ideas to consider:

- **Vocal Storytelling**: Share your stories, wisdom, and life lessons through vocal storytelling. Sit down with family members and friends and narrate your life experiences. Record these sessions to preserve them for future generations. Vocal storytelling is a profound way to connect with your loved ones and impart your knowledge.

- **Writing or Journaling**: Writing is a powerful medium for capturing your thoughts, experiences, and personal philosophy. Consider keeping a journal, writing letters, or even authoring a memoir. Your written words can provide invaluable insights for your family and offer a glimpse into your personality and beliefs.

- **Video/Photo Montage**: Compile a video or photo montage that encapsulates the significant moments of your life. This could be an emotionally rich experience for your family, providing a visual representation of your legacy. Include photos and videos of important milestones, family gatherings, and cherished memories.

- **Donations**: Support causes and organizations that align with your values. Consider charitable donations as a way to make a difference in the world and leave a legacy of benevolence. Whether it's contributing to education, healthcare, the arts, or environmental conservation, your donations can continue to benefit others long after you're gone.

Leaving a legacy isn't just about imparting your wisdom; it's also an opportunity to foster communication in numerous ways. It's a chance to create deeper connections with your family and friends. You foster a sense of unity and belonging within your family by sharing your stories, values, and life lessons. Moreover, knowing you're leaving a lasting mark can bring you immense satisfaction and a profound sense of fulfillment. Your legacy can continue to positively impact your loved ones, even after you're no longer here, ensuring that your values and principles endure for generations to come.

Estate Planning

Estate planning is a comprehensive process that involves managing and organizing your assets, property, and personal affairs during your lifetime and distributing those assets upon your death. It's a strategic, proactive approach to ensuring that your financial and personal goals are met while you're alive and after you pass away. Estate planning goes beyond simply drafting a will; it encompasses various legal tools and documents that help you control your assets and make informed decisions regarding your healthcare and financial matters. We'll review all these essential documents and legal tools later. For now, you need to gain a better appreciation for the essence of estate planning. Here are a few important reasons as to why you should consider taking your estate planning journey more seriously:

- **Protecting Assets**: Estate planning helps protect your assets, ensuring they are distributed according to your wishes. Without a well-structured plan, your assets might be subject to costly probate, and this process can lead to delays, expenses, and potential disputes among your heirs. With proper estate planning, you can minimize estate taxes and ensure your loved ones receive their inheritance promptly and efficiently.

- **Ensuring Wishes are Fulfilled**: Estate planning allows you to specify your exact preferences for the distribution of your assets. It ensures that your loved ones receive the inheritances you want to leave them and that any philanthropic or charitable contributions you intend to make are executed as you desire. Estate planning provides clear directives to your family, minimizing potential disagreements or confusion regarding your intentions.

- **Other Legal Considerations**: Estate planning encompasses various legal considerations beyond asset distribution. It involves designating guardians for minor children, appointing individuals to make medical and financial decisions if you become incapacitated and outlining your preferences for end-of-life care. Estate planning ensures that all legal aspects of your life are well-documented and that your values are preserved if you cannot express them yourself.

In essence, estate planning is about taking control of your financial, personal, and healthcare decisions, ensuring your wishes are carried out and your assets are protected. It allows you to leave a well-structured, organized legacy that reflects your values and priorities while minimizing the potential for legal complications and family disputes.

Creating Essential Documents

Wills

A last will and testament, commonly referred to as a will, is a fundamental legal document that outlines your final wishes regarding the distribution of your assets and property after your passing. It is an essential component of estate planning and can be created by individuals who meet specific legal requirements.

To create a will, you must typically be of sound mind and above a certain age, often 18 years old. Being of sound mind means you understand the nature and extent of your property and the implications of creating a will. Your will may be challenged if you lack the mental capacity to comprehend these elements.

There are several reasons why people create wills, such as:

- **Asset Distribution**: A will allows you to specify how your assets should be distributed among your beneficiaries upon your death.

- **Guardianship for Minor Children**: If you have minor children, a will allows you to designate a guardian who will be responsible for their care in the event of your death.

- **Executor Appointment**: You can nominate an executor to carry out the instructions in your will, ensuring your estate is managed according to your wishes.

- **Charitable Giving:** Wills provide a mechanism for leaving assets to charitable organizations or causes you care about.

- **Pet Care**: In some jurisdictions, you can use your will to designate someone to take care of your pets after your death.

Ultimately, a will gives you control over who receives your property, assets, and possessions after your passing. Also, if you pass away without a valid will (intestate), your assets may be distributed according to state laws, which might not align with your preferences. A will ensures your assets are distributed as you wish. In cases wherein you have minor children, a will allows you to specify who will become their guardian if both parents pass away. You can also nominate a trusted individual to manage your estate's affairs, simplifying the estate settlement process. In the end, a well-drafted will can help prevent family disputes and legal conflicts over asset distribution.

The registration of a will varies by jurisdiction. In some places, wills must be registered with the local probate court; in others, registration might not be mandatory. Registering your will can provide additional protection against loss or damage and help your beneficiaries locate the document when needed.

Working with a qualified attorney when drafting your will is essential, ensuring it complies with your jurisdiction's legal requirements and serves your unique estate planning needs. Your attorney can guide you through the process and help you understand the specific rules and procedures related to will creation and registration in your area.

Trusts

Trusts are essential tools in estate planning, allowing individuals to manage and distribute their assets in a way that aligns with their specialized financial and personal objectives. A trust is a legal entity that holds and manages assets on behalf of beneficiaries according to the instructions laid out in a trust document. Regarding the benefits of trusts, certain trusts can shield assets from creditors and legal claims. Also, assets held in a trust may bypass the probate process, speeding up asset distribution and reducing associated costs. Lastly, trusts enable the grantor to define specific terms and conditions for asset distribution, even after their passing.

Unlike wills, trust agreements are generally private documents that don't become part of public records. A will outlines how your assets should be distributed upon your death, which goes into effect only after you pass away. Wills go through the probate process, which can be public, costly, and time-consuming.

There are numerous types of trusts, but some of the most common ones include:

- **Revocable Living Trust (RLT)**: Also known as a living trust, this trust allows the grantor to maintain control over their assets during their lifetime. It can be altered or revoked at any time. When the grantor passes away, assets in the trust are typically distributed to beneficiaries without going through probate.

- **Irrevocable Trust**: In contrast to a revocable trust, assets placed in an irrevocable trust cannot be modified or revoked by the grantor. This type of trust is often used for asset protection, reducing estate tax liability, and qualifying for government benefits.

- **Testamentary Trust**: Created through a will, this trust only becomes effective upon the grantor's death. It is used to address specific issues, such as managing assets for minor children or providing for a surviving spouse.

- **Charitable Remainder Trust (CRT)**:This trust allows the grantor to donate assets to a charity while retaining income generated by those assets during their lifetime. After the grantor's death, the remaining assets go to the designated charity.

- **Special Needs Trust (SNT)**:Designed to benefit individuals with disabilities, an SNT ensures that beneficiaries can receive financial support without affecting their eligibility for government assistance programs.

- **Generation-Skipping Trust (GST)**: A GST is created to transfer assets to beneficiaries who are at least two generations younger than the grantor. This can help reduce estate taxes and provide for grandchildren or more distant descendants.

These are some of the key aspects of trusts in estate planning. Different types of trusts serve various purposes, and their appropriateness depends on individual goals and circumstances. As with any other major legal decision in retirement, it's always best to consult an experienced estate planning attorney to determine the most suitable trust strategy for your needs.

Power of Attorney

A Power of Attorney is a legal tool that allows the principal to designate someone they trust to manage their affairs in case they become unable to do so due to illness, injury, or other circumstances. This authority can cover a variety of matters, including financial, legal, and healthcare decisions. There are different ways through which this can be manifested, such as:

- **General Power of Attorney**:This grants broad authority to the agent to handle various financial and legal matters on behalf of the principal. It is often used for short-term situations or when the principal needs assistance but remains mentally capable.

- **Durable Power of Attorney**:This type remains effective even if the principal becomes mentally incapacitated. It gives the agent the authority to make decisions on behalf of the principal in the event of incapacity.

- **Limited (or Specific) Power of Attorney**:This document grants authority for specific and limited actions, often related to a particular transaction or event, such as selling a property or managing investments.

- **Healthcare Power of Attorney (Medical Power of Attorney)**: This document authorizes the agent to make healthcare decisions for the principal if they are unable to do so. It is often used in conjunction with an Advance Healthcare Directive or Living Will.

- **Springing Power of Attorney**: This type "springs" into effect only upon a specific event, typically the principal's incapacity. It is often used when the principal wants to maintain control until a triggering event occurs.

The agent's responsibilities are outlined in the Power of Attorney document. Depending on the document's terms, these responsibilities can include managing financial assets, paying bills, making legal decisions, and handling healthcare choices. The agent is obligated to act in the principal's best interests, maintain accurate records, and avoid any conflicts of interest.

Selecting the right agent is a crucial decision. The agent should be someone trustworthy, reliable, and capable of handling the responsibilities outlined in the document. Many people choose family members, close friends, or legal professionals as their agents. A Power of Attorney is a valuable tool in estate planning that allows individuals to designate a trusted agent to act on their behalf in various capacities. It provides flexibility in managing financial, legal, and healthcare matters while offering peace of mind and protection.

Healthcare Directives

A healthcare directive is a legally binding document outlining a person's medical care and end-of-life preferences. It specifies the treatments they desire or refuse, designates a healthcare agent (also known as a healthcare proxy or attorney-in-fact) to make medical decisions on their behalf, and communicates their values and choices regarding healthcare.

Healthcare directives give individuals the autonomy to make decisions about their medical care and ensure their wishes are respected. Having written instructions in a healthcare directive can help prevent disagreements among family members about medical decisions. In many cases, healthcare agents are appointed to make difficult decisions on behalf of the individual, relieving family members of the emotional burden of deciding what is in the patient's best interest. Healthcare directives allow individuals to express their preferences regarding life-sustaining treatments and the level of care they want in a terminal condition.

Healthcare directives are subject to state laws and regulations. While there is a degree of uniformity across the United States, the specific requirements and terminology may vary from state to state. Creating a healthcare directive that complies with the legal standards of the individual's state of residence is essential.

Estate Planning Checklist

Okay, that might have been a lot to take in. But that's fine. You have plenty of time to process and prepare all of these things. For your benefit, here's a quick rundown of essential documents for estate planning. It's important to note that while these documents can be highly beneficial for many individuals, estate planning is a highly personal process, and the need for specific documents may vary depending on individual circumstances and legal requirements. Consultation with a qualified attorney or estate planning professional is essential to tailor the plan to your specific situation:

- **Last Will and Testament**: This document outlines how you want your assets distributed after passing. It also allows you to appoint an executor to oversee the distribution.

- **Revocable Living Trust**:This trust allows you to manage your assets during your lifetime and allows for asset distribution upon your incapacity or passing. It can help avoid the probate process.

- **Irrevocable Trust**:This type of trust transfers assets out of your estate to minimize estate taxes or protect assets for specific beneficiaries.

- **Durable Power of Attorney (POA)**:This document designates an agent to make financial decisions on your behalf if you become incapacitated.

- **Healthcare Power of Attorney**: Designate a trusted individual to make healthcare decisions on your behalf if you are unable to do so.

- **Beneficiary Designations**:Ensure that beneficiary designations on retirement accounts, life insurance, and other accounts are up to date and aligned with your estate plan.

- **Guardianship Designation**: If you have minor children, you can designate a legal guardian in your will to take care of them if you and the other parent cannot.

- **Digital Asset Plan**: A plan for managing and distributing digital assets, including online accounts and digital files.

- **Tax Planning Documents**: Documents to help minimize estate taxes, such as Family Limited Partnerships or Charitable Remainder Trusts.

- **Property Ownership Records**: Documentation of property ownership, deeds, and titles.

- **Business Succession Plan**: If you own a business, a plan for the future management or sale of the business.

- **Memorial Instructions**: Instructions for your funeral or memorial service, including any specific wishes you may have.

Please note that this checklist provides an overview of potential estate planning documents. Your specific needs may vary, and it's best to consult with family and a legal expert to determine the best path forward for you regarding estate planning.

Wealth Transfer Strategies

Wealth transfer, in the context of estate planning, refers to the process of transferring assets, property, and wealth from one generation to the next, typically upon an individual's death. Wealth transfer aims to facilitate the smooth transition of assets to intended beneficiaries, minimize estate taxes, protect assets, and leave a lasting legacy.

Now, there are a few different ways you can go about transferring your wealth when you leave this world, such as gifting, inheritance, or just plain charitable donations. Gifting is the process of transferring assets during one's lifetime. Inheritance occurs when assets are transferred through a will or trust after an individual's death. Gifting can reduce the size of the taxable estate and potentially reduce estate taxes. Incorporating charitable giving into wealth transfer can be a valuable strategy. By leaving assets to charitable organizations, you can achieve tax benefits and support causes you are passionate about.

Chapter Conclusion

The idea of bequeathing your wealth and leaving behind a legacy can be a touchy subject to broach while you're still alive but ironing these details out before your passing is essential. Even though this might be difficult, here are various strategies you can employ to make this process smoother and easier:

- **Family Communication**: Effective communication with family members is critical to wealth transfer. Openly discussing your estate plan, wishes, and intentions with your loved ones can prevent misunderstandings, disputes, and potential family conflicts. Encouraging dialogue and understanding among family members can foster cooperation and support throughout the wealth transfer process.

- **Gift Planning**: Gifting can be a tax-efficient wealth transfer strategy. The annual gift tax exclusion allows individuals to gift a certain amount to each recipient tax-free. Additionally, larger lifetime gifts can be made while potentially reducing overall estate taxes.

- **Use of Trusts**: Establishing trusts can offer various benefits for wealth transfer. Irrevocable trusts, for instance, can remove assets from your taxable estate while still allowing you to benefit from the income generated by those assets during your lifetime. Trusts can also provide for beneficiaries' ongoing care and support and protect assets from creditors and legal claims.

- **Life Insurance**: Life insurance can be an effective wealth transfer tool. A life insurance policy can provide a tax-free death benefit, which can be used to pay estate taxes, equalize inheritances among heirs, or support charitable giving.

- **Legal Documents**: Ensure you have a well-structured estate plan that includes a will, trusts, and advanced directives. These documents are essential to specify your wealth transfer and asset distribution intentions.

Working with financial and legal professionals is crucial to determining the most appropriate wealth transfer strategies for your particular financial situation and family dynamics. Estate planning should be a dynamic process that evolves as circumstances change. Open family communication about your wishes and intentions can help create a successful wealth transfer strategy.

Conclusion

As we conclude this book, the main message shines clear: Retirement is not just about reaching a milestone; it's about stepping into a new and exciting chapter of life. Your retirement years can be filled with purpose, passion, and fulfillment. It's not merely the end of one journey but the beginning of another. Retirement is a time to rediscover your passions, explore new horizons, and make a difference in your life and the lives of others. And throughout this process, planning can be your essential best friend. Create a roadmap for your retirement that aligns with your dreams and values. This is the best way to make the most out of the next phase of your life. Whether you're embarking on new adventures, focusing on your health, or sharing your wisdom and wealth, retirement offers opportunities for personal growth, joy, and making lasting memories.

Ultimately, I wish you to experience the same sense of purpose, accomplishment, and happiness in your retirement journey that so many others have enjoyed in the twilight years of their lives. You deserve it. You live a happy, healthy, and honest life and deserve to culminate it in the grandest way possible. And it's essential that you get started on the planning process as soon as possible!

Here's a secret about time—it tends to slip away when you're not looking. So, don't let the busyness of life or the worries of tomorrow deter you from taking that first step. Each sunrise is an opportunity to step into the grand adventure of retirement. Embrace this very moment, for it carries the promise of new experiences, new connections, and new growth.

Every day offers the chance to rekindle a passion, to make new friends, and to explore uncharted territories. Life in retirement is like a garden; the earlier you plant the seeds, the more abundant the harvest.

I would like to express my gratitude to you, the reader, for accompanying me on this journey through the world of retirement. Your feedback is invaluable. If you find this book helpful, please consider leaving a review, as it can help others embark on their path to a fulfilling retirement.

Retirement is not the end; it's the beginning of a new adventure. May your retirement be filled with happiness, prosperity, and the joy of making a lasting impact on the world. Cheers to your incredible journey ahead!

Companion Books You Might Enjoy:

Life After Work: The Bucket List Book

This bucket list book helps you **brainstorm, categorize, prioritize, and plan** your personal bucket list.

Included in this book are planning pages to assist you to:

- reflect on your **passions**
- consider your **dreams** and **goals**
- identify the physical, financial, emotional/spiritual, relationship, time and logistical planning elements for your list

and more!

Life After Work: The Bucket List Book

https://www.amazon.com/dp/B0CQNYNWV7

Life After Work: Retirement Daily Agenda

Each page in this agenda includes sections for you to:

- pursue your **passions**
- stay **active**
- be **social**
- record appointments

And more!

Life After Work: Retirement Daily Agenda

https://www.amazon.com/dp/B0CQNX6ZSB

REFERENCES

Bouldin, T. (2022, May 6). *How to streamline your wardrobe for retirement*. Baltimore Style. https://www.baltimorestyle.com/how-to-streamline-your-wardrobe-for-retirement/

Coursolle, K. M., Sweeney, M. M., Raymo, J. M., & Ho, J.-H. (2010). The association between retirement and emotional well-being: Does prior work-family conflict matter? *The Journals of Gerontology Series B: Psychological Sciences and Social Sciences, 65B*(5), 609–620. https://doi.org/10.1093/geronb/gbp116

Curtis, G. (2022, February 27). *6 estate planning must-haves*. Investopedia. https://www.investopedia.com/articles/pf/07/estate_plan_checklist.asp

Eisenberg, R. (2013, October 23). *Time management is crucial to a happy retirement*. Forbes. https://www.forbes.com/sites/nextavenue/2013/10/23/time-management-is-crucial-to-a-happy-retirement/?sh=2f8eb6666dce

Fontinelle, A. (2023, July 26). *Retirement uses for your health savings account (HSA)*. Investopedia. https://www.investopedia.com/articles/personal-finance/091615/how-use-your-hsa-retirement.asp

Galanti, D. (2022, October 23). *6 ways to find a new passion after retirement*. Goldsteins' Rosenberg's Raphael-Sacks. https://www.goldsteinsfu neral.com/6-ways-to-find-a-new-passion-after-retirement/

Ganti, A. (2023, March 9). *Net worth*. Investopedia. https://www.inv estopedia.com/terms/n/networth.asp

Greenview Team. (2023, June 23). *Embracing retirement: Adjusting to the first month of freedom*. Greenview Park Retirement Village. https://greenviewpark.co.nz/embracing-retirement-adjusting-to-th e-first-month-of-freedom/

How to create a meaningful life legacy. (n.d.). Era Living. https://www .eraliving.com/blog/how-to-create-a-meaningful-life-legacy/

Jespersen, C. (2020, December 15). *5 steps for tracking your monthly expenses*. NerdWallet. https://www.nerdwallet.com/article/finance/trac king-monthly-expenses

Kagan, J. (2019). *Social security*. Investopedia. https://www.investope dia.com/terms/s/socialsecurity.asp

Kagan, J. (2022, January 3). *Individual retirement account (IRA)*. Investopedia. https://www.investopedia.com/terms/i/ira.asp

Lagemann, J. (2023, June 12). *11 meaningful ways older adults can volunteer right now*. Forbes Health. https://www.forbes.com/health/he althy-aging/volunteer-opportunities-for-older-adults/

Lake, R. (2019). *How inflation eats away at your retirement*. Investopedia. https://www.investopedia.com/articles/retirement/052616/how-inf lation-eats-away-your-retirement.asp

LaPonsie, M. (2020). *7 housing options for seniors*. U.S. News & World Report. https://money.usnews.com/money/retirement/articles/housing -options-for-seniors

McDermott, N. (2022, April 7). *What is a retirement home?* Forbes Health. https://www.forbes.com/health/healthy-aging/what-is-a-retirement-home/

Miller, M. (2022, March 25). What retirement means for your taxes. *The New York Times.* https://www.nytimes.com/2022/03/25/business/retirement-taxes-social-security.html

Morah, C. (2021, June 13). *Evaluating your personal financial statement.* Investopedia. https://www.investopedia.com/articles/pf/08/evaluate-personal-financial-statement.asp

O'Shea, B., & Schwahn, L. (2021, January 13). *Budgeting 101: How to budget money.* NerdWallet. https://www.nerdwallet.com/article/finance/how-to-budget

Reed, D. (2022, June 8). *Preparing for the next chapter - retirement.* The Retirement Advice Centre. http://www.smartretirement.com.au/preparing-for-the-next-chapter-retirement/

Shapira, J. A. (2019, November 26). *How to dress your age: Balancing style with maturity.* Gentleman's Gazette. https://www.gentlemansgazette.com/how-to-dress-your-age/

7 reasons why seniors should learn a new hobby in retirement. (2023, August 17). IntegraCare. https://www.integracare.com/7-reasons-why-seniors-should-learn-a-new-hobby-in-retirement/

Straight talk about financial planning for your retirement. (n.d.). Office of the New York State Comptroller. https://www.osc.state.ny.us/retirement/publications/straight-talk-about-financial-planning-your-retirement

Ullman, M. (2021, October 23). *Want to travel the world in retirement? Here's how.* Investopedia. https://www.investopedia.com/articles/personal-finance/102214/want-travel-world-retirement-heres-how.asp

Volunteering & retirees: Types, organizations and benefits. (n.d.). RetireGuide. https://www.retireguide.com/retirement-life-leisure/volunte ering/

Walker, C. (2023, January 9). *Friendships in retirement: 7 easy ways to make relationships.* Cumberland Crossing by OceanView. https://www.cumberlandcrossingrc.com/news/7-easy-ways-make -friends-during-retirement-years/

Walker, R. (2019, September 8). *10 unexpected benefits of dressing well.* The Rachel Review. https://www.therachelreview.com/10-unexpected -benefits-of-dressing-well/

Weaver, E. (2023, January 12). *The best activities that help keep your mind sharp in retirement.* Monroe Village. https://monroevillageonline.org/n ews/the-best-activities-that-help-keep-your-mind-sharp-in-retirement/

What to wear in retirement: 8 must-know tips! (2023, April 1). Shopping on Champagne. https://www.shoppingonchampagne.com/blog/what-t o-wear-in-retirement

Wooll, M. (2022, February 2). *How to find your passion and discover your zest for life.* BetterUp. https://www.betterup.com/blog/how-to-find-yo ur-passion

Printed in Great Britain
by Amazon

36250441R00089